COLOR

Latino Voices in the Pacific Northwest

D1376828

COLOR

Latino Voices in the Pacific Northwest

Lorane A. West

PROPERTY OF
BAKER COLLEGE
Owosso Campus

WSU
PRESS

Washington State University Press
Pullman, Washington

Washington State University Press
PO Box 645910
Pullman, Washington 99164-5910
Phone: 800-354-7360
Fax: 509-335-8568
E-mail: wsupress@wsu.edu
Web site: wsupress.wsu.edu

© 2004 by the Board of Regents of Washington State University
All rights reserved
First printing 2004

Printed and bound in the United States of America on pH neutral, acid-free paper.
Reproduction or transmission of material contained in this publication in excess of
that permitted by copyright law is prohibited without permission in writing from
the publisher.

Library of Congress Cataloging-in-Publication Data

West, Lorane A., 1960–
    Color : Latino voices in the Pacific Northwest / Lorane A. West.
      p. cm.
    ISBN 0-87422-274-5 (alk. paper)
    1. Hispanic Americans—Northwest, Pacific—Interviews. 2. Hispanic Ameri-
cans—Northwest, Pacific—Social conditions. 3. Northwest, Pacific—Social
conditions. 4. Northwest, Pacific—Ethnic relations. 5. Northwest, Pacific—
Biography. I. Title.

F855.2.S75W47 2004
979.5'00468073—dc22   2004008737

Fine Quality Books from the Pacific Northwest

Table of Contents

Foreword

I come from an immigrant family and married into an immigrant family. I maintain ties with my ancestral village in Finland and speak Swedish with my relatives. I worked for three years as a Russian interpreter living onboard Soviet ships in the Pacific Ocean and the Bering Sea. I have spent the last twenty years with my Salvadoran husband, and we speak both English and Spanish at home. Now settled in the United States, we have lived in Nicaragua and El Salvador. In both countries, I flew in with money in the bank and a college education, and was able to obtain legal residence status fairly easily. Even so, as a recent arrival, I experienced deep loneliness and numbing isolation.

I have not experienced walking into another country under cover of night being led by a man to whom I have paid six months wages in cash, who might leave me lost along the way. I have not experienced traveling two thousand miles from home to get a minimum wage job, only able to provide my children with food and shelter by leaving them behind. Or waiting years to reunite with my husband, who works in another country and sends me money, to discover that he has started a new family during his lonely exile. I have not experienced giving up on my own dreams so I can keep younger siblings in school. But my clients have experienced this and many other things in their travels.

As a Spanish interpreter in the medical setting, I am favored with daily opportunities to participate in the lives of my immigrant patients in an intimate and personal setting. I spend countless waiting room hours with my patients, getting to know them and hearing about their lives in the United States. I go into the exam room with them, observe some of their surgeries, and assist them as they learn to live with chronic illness. I follow them through cancer treatments, pregnancies, births, and deaths. And I hear my patients' stories. The idea for this book stems from their stories.

Each story is written in English as a loosely translated spoken monologue from the immigrant's perspective. I want to emphasize that no story is based exactly on a given individual's specific experience. The ideas for stories I have gathered over the years have changed form and character to become what is fairly classed as fiction. The best fiction should ring true, but if you expect to find an identifiable client of mine in this book, you will be mistaken. Without claiming to speak on anyone's behalf, this book offers a unique glimpse into the rarely seen world of the recent immigrant. It also provides some insights into the modern healthcare delivery system and other matters of cultural interest.

I have written this book out of love, gratitude, respect, and admiration for my clients: Spanish-speaking immigrants living and working in the Pacific Northwest.

Dedication

I dedicate this book to:

my mother, Dharlene Elaine West,
who taught me to read and write in English;

my father, Hans Börje Westö, AKA Bob West,
who taught me to laugh in Swedish;

my husband, Enrique Patiño Burch,
who taught me to love in Spanish;

my children, Anna Luisa and Miguel Enrique Patiño West;

and to immigrants, refugees, travelers, and lost souls.

You are not alone.

—Lorane Alisa West

Adoption

Now that my husband understands we can never have children, he has said we should think about adopting. When I first found out I would have to undergo this hysterectomy, I told him I was sorry. I told him, if you need to have children of your own flesh, go out and find a woman to bear your children, then bring them home to me. I will be humble about it, not angry. God knows my heart. I would never beat them like some stepmothers do. I would love them as if they were my own, because they would be yours. I understand if you need this.

I know you would never beat them, my husband told me. But I don't want my own children. If God willed that you lose your womb, then it is not His will for me to have children of my own, either, because I am your husband. I'm not having children without you, he said.

You are the only woman I ever want, my husband told me. And he really means it. I'm lucky that way, because he has a brother; what a skirt chaser! I told his brother, if you put a skirt on a broomstick, you would probably try to be with the broom, you are just that careless. But when I met my husband's family, they said I was lucky because my husband had never had a girlfriend before me. And I told them, he is my first boyfriend also; even though I am not a young girl, I have never had a boyfriend, either. We are each other's first.

So even though I have had this surgery, my husband assures me that everything will remain the same between us, except he plans to love me even more because I suffered this loss through him, he says, because he impregnated me and I lost my womb, so he says he would never ever want to leave me or replace me. My fate is his fate, he tells me.

Anyway, the doctors asked me to let them know if I had any other questions before you left, so I guess our main question is this: Can anyone here help us find out how to adopt a baby? Because it looks like my husband is planning to stay with me, even though I can't bear any children. And it looks like he doesn't want to go out and have his own children without me. So it looks like we're going to stay together for all our lives, and since all this is true, we'd like to adopt a baby or two. That way the children will belong to both of us equally.

I thought when I lost my womb, that would be the end of it, but my husband tells me I'm crazy and stupid. Why would I care about your womb, he told me, I've never even seen it. You're the one I like to look at, you silly little thing, your pretty face and smiling eyes and your curly, curly hair that's always a big mess. You're the one I love. Didn't you say that, honey? What are you laughing at? You know you did. Just admit it! Now tell the interpreter!

1

Alone

I've never been alone before. In Guatemala, you just never are. Everywhere you go, someone goes with you. You are always accompanied, especially in public. You go to the store, you run your errands, you visit a relative, you take a bus, you always, always take along a companion, you see. It's just a custom we have, to never be alone. So when I ended up alone here, and my husband was deported, I can't tell you how traumatized I was.

Now I am alone. My husband is deported, and he cannot return within five years or he can be sent to federal prison. Even after that, he will never be able to get legal papers to stay here, because under the new laws, if you're deported, you can never become a legal immigrant. He didn't commit a real crime, but now with Bush and the thing in New York, I guess they made it a crime just to be here without the right papers. Just being here is like burglary or robbery.

The reason we were here was to save up money and buy a business in Guatemala. We lived very cheaply, and we were working hard. My husband got me a job at the same building where he worked, cleaning offices. It's a good job, but then they had the INS raid, and he was captured and deported. Thank God I was in the bathroom during the raid! They didn't get me.

Except all of a sudden I went from going everywhere with my husband—to work, the store, to bed, to the park—I went from that to going everywhere alone. I don't have any friends or family, and I've been going to church, but the last thing most people want is one more sad and lonely person to take care of. So I have our apartment with the rent due, and I have to find some female roommates and another part-time job quickly, but this time I have to do it all alone, and I don't even know how to start. I've honestly never been alone in my life.

I've heard white people like to be alone. You see them walking around mostly alone or eating alone in restaurants, shopping alone, driving alone, even going to movies alone. But we Latinos, we like to be together. I feel safer that way, not just here, but everywhere. How nice it feels to be waiting for a bus and turn and have someone you know to exchange a few words with. How wonderful to ask someone in the store, hey, do you remember if we need more limes? How sweet it is to have a husband, brother, friend, or son to accompany you everywhere and help you with things, and to never ever be alone. Just to be accompanied!

I've heard white people only know that feeling once. When they are children, they are allowed to have a best friend. But when they grow up, they are supposed to quit doing that and just be alone all the time. I frankly don't know how they can stand it. How they must suffer.

Alzheimer's

Yes, I take care of my old wifey. They didn't want me to; they said once someone loses her memory, you have to put her in an institution. But I said there was no way I was going to farm my dear old sweetheart out like she was an old horse. Animals, you put out to pasture. People, you don't put out to pasture. Some people might be put in an institution, but not my wife, no ma'am. And with no wish to offend, you can tell them that from me.

They gave me all these excuses about why I should put her away. Like, they can feed her, they can keep her from going outside and getting lost, they can have someone watching her all the time. They can have fun activities for her, like bingo or something. But the whole thing, if you ask me, is just plain wrong. My little lady is not going to buy it, she's not going to like it, she's not going to go! She would be miserable beyond belief.

She needs feeding? I can feed her! You think I don't know how to hold a spoon? I've been feeding myself for years without any problems; I think I can figure out how to get a spoon to her mouth! Plus I know what she likes to eat, since we've been eating the same meals for sixty-two years. Anything I like, she likes, so I can make sure she will enjoy her food.

She needs fun things to do? Well, guess what? She doesn't play bingo or any of those games. And she doesn't like to watch television, either, like everyone was doing in that home they had us go visit. She just likes to listen to our kind of music and visit with our family and potter around the house doing all the usual things she has liked to do for years, making the bed, sweeping, cleaning, and that kind of thing. So what if she makes the bed three times? She enjoys it. I take her out to the park, grocery shopping, and all kinds of things.

Then they tried to tell me, but if your relative, your loved one, is losing the mental end of things, she could wander away. You could take a shower, and she could walk out of the house and disappear. No, I told them, she won't, because I'll tie her down. They tie people down in the institution, anyway, so I might as well just tie her down at home. She has a good life with me. Sure, she's forgetful, but that's no reason to lock someone up, especially my dear little wife who has been my helpmeet for all these years.

I appreciate the doctors, I know they don't mean any harm. They just really believe in sending people away; they really believe the sick people are well cared for in those institutions. But I just don't believe it. The only way I could know for sure how she is being cared for is to care for her myself. That is what *in sickness and in health* means. That is what I promised.

Anesthesia

That time where they gave me too much anesthesia and they couldn't get me to wake up? Well, I dreamed I was on a stormy sea in a huge ship, and it all seemed very real, like when I was a sailor. There was fog all around, and each wave would crash over the deck, almost sinking the ship, and then the captain was ordering me to get the water off the deck. It was my job to save us from sinking and drowning, but I had to use this motorized pump that worked backwards, like a leaf blower, and each wave filled the deck up with water, and we started to go down, and then I would get the leaf blower thing going and get the water off the deck, but it kept sputtering out, and then the ship would be ready to go down, and in the midst of all this noise and the wind and the waves and the captain yelling at me, I heard my mother calling my name.

I heard her calling my name as clear as day, but I couldn't figure out where she was calling from. I looked all around the ship, but she wasn't there. So between waves I climbed up to the prow and looked out into the fog, and I could barely discern through the white of the fog a little rowboat, and in it was my mother of all people, rowing furiously with huge oars and almost going under with each huge wave! And she called out to me, save me! Help me! Save me! And I yelled to the captain, you have to change direction, you have to turn this ship around, you have to get to that rowboat, that's my mother in it, and we have to save her!

He turned the ship around and we got up alongside her in the rowboat, but every time I reached out to her, another wave would come and she would get pulled away and I couldn't reach her, but I kept reaching out over the side, leaning so far I almost fell out. You know how the boats go up and down so one minute the rowboat was above me, and then it was down in a trough? Finally, I managed to just pull her up onto deck, and she cried my name. I shut my eyes in my joy and held her hand tight. When I opened my eyes, I was in the hospital bed, and she was holding my hand and calling out my name, looking right into my face as she held my hand.

You see, the doctor told my family that they couldn't wake me up, and the only hope to call me back to this life was to get someone in there who is a beloved person, like a mother, wife, sister—someone very beloved whose voice is well known who can call me back to this life from beyond. So they chose my mother, because we have always been so close, and she came and she called me. And it's funny like that, because you want to save someone, and then they save you. I'm sure I would have died if she hadn't come in that rowboat into my stormy dream.

4

Animal

I don't know if God is punishing me for past deeds, but before this back injury, I treated my wife like an animal. I used her poorly, there's no denying it. I used to ask her for my marital rights three, sometimes four times a day. She never denied me; she knew it was her duty. That went on for years. She was pregnant seven times and had the five surviving children in a row.

After eight years of marriage, she shyly told me her woman's doctor, he wanted to meet with us together. So I went with her to the appointment. The doctor told me, he said, listen, your wife is a decent lady. You can't use her like that. You've worn her to the bone. You're killing her slowly. She's coming apart down there. She's dripping all the time. She's had no time to heal. What's wrong with you? You can't keep this up, or as a doctor I'm telling you, you'll kill her and raise those children alone. Leave her alone, he told me.

Well, my wife, she just sat there looking embarrassed. I was embarrassed, too. I told him, doctor, I love my wife, but what can I do? I'm a healthy man. I work very hard on the farm all the time, tending the fields and the cattle. There's so much work to do. A man needs to relax, too, not just work like a dog and have no pleasure. I want to be close to my wife, and I need the relief. I only do it because I love her. What can I do?

Well, the doctor, he said, listen, why don't you find some nice, clean girl and release yourself that way. Honestly, as a doctor I'm telling you, your wife can't keep this up. She won't live through it. My wife, she just sat there saying nothing, so I guess she agreed. Well, I didn't have much choice. I ended up finding a nice, clean girl or two, and next thing you know, I had married women coming to me. They talk amongst themselves, women do, so word got around.

My wife never acted jealous. What she might have felt in her heart, I'll never know, but she never said a single word to me about it. When a woman would get crazy about me and call our home, she would just hand me the phone and let it be my business. My wife is such a decent soul. We kept on having relations, but just once a week on Saturday nights, and very gently.

Then we moved here, and I had the accident at work. Now I am in horrible pain, and God help me, but I can't pleasure my wife at all. Can't perform my marital duty, not even once a week. Can't feel a thing except my pain. She has to work to help support us now. And I found out how it feels to have her going out and working all day, leaving me to worry about whom she meets, who will please her in the way I can't. I won't say a word about it if she ends up taking a lover; I know I deserve it, but I still pray that she will be faithful. God forgive me my weakness.

Argentina

We have a funny split in our family, because my wife loves being a North American; she thinks it is just so great here, and I am very much an Argentinean and will not change, while our older son is really more North American than South American, and our younger son is more Argentinean than any Argentinean, even though he is the only one of us who was born in the United States. I think a lot of families have this split, just based on personalities, I guess.

My younger son, he has the flag of Argentina on his wall. He has travel posters of our most beautiful places—our mountains and lakes, our major cities and tourist attractions. He reads all the literature from the major South American writers, and he doesn't plan to move out when he turns eighteen like boys here do. All he wants to do is move back to Argentina with us.

My older son, he is the opposite. He moved out of the house, not to marry, which is our tradition, but just to move out! He speaks Spanish with an accent, although he lived in Argentina until he was seven. I can't understand how he has lost so much. All his friends have been English-speaking, and he hardly wants to speak Spanish even to his own mother, who doesn't speak English well, although she loves this country so much.

When my older son turned fifteen, I took him on his first trip back home. We spent a month, and on the last day, I took him by taxi to a lookout point in the city and said, son, look around. Take a good look around at your country. I am old, and I would like to retire here soon. Is this a place where you think you could make your future? It was a solemn moment for me; I felt like I was offering him my world, but he just said, Dad, it's nice and all that, but you took me to live somewhere else, and that is where I feel at home now. To be honest, Dad, I love you and all that, but I don't feel that comfortable here. The United States is my home now.

When we got back to the United States, I talked to my wife about it, thinking she would sympathize with me in my loss, but she just hugged me and laughed. She said, honey, we live in the United States now. Argentina is our old home, but this is our new home. Argentina is a place to visit now. But for me, madam, it is not a place to visit; it is my home. You could slice me up for dinner and fry me in butter and I would still be Argentinean; no one and nothing can take that away. Sometimes I just wish I had not let my wife convince me that the boys would have a better chance if we brought them here to go to school. What's better? We don't even have a place in this world where we all four want to live anymore. We have no real country now. No offense, but this country doesn't count. It's like everywhere and nowhere together.

Arthritis

I know I am old, and I want to be grateful, but this arthritis is hard for me to handle. It is the cause of so many difficulties and limitations in my life. I try not to show it; I keep up with my household duties, thank God, but the children and grandchildren and even my husband all notice it. I can't walk the right way any more. I limp, and I walk bowlegged.

I am limping more now because we're expecting some guests from Peru; my sister's son and his family, they're coming up to visit next week. They told me on the phone, they said, don't fix anything up for us, we will be fine, just relax and enjoy our visit. But you know how we Latinos are. We have to make them feel welcome, and that means a spotless home.

My husband and I, we have been scrubbing and cleaning cabinets and shaking out rugs and dusting. We have to get enough pillows and blankets set up. My children said to just get sleeping bags, but I don't think they would consider it polite to be offered sleeping bags; they wouldn't be used to that kind of treatment. Of course, we will give up our room for my sister's son and his wife; that is our tradition. So my husband and I will sleep on the old couch.

Anyway, the doctor is talking to me about hip replacement. He says the sockets are all worn out. My knees and ankles hurt so much, too. I guess being close to ninety years old doesn't help me much, either. My husband and I used to love to go dancing. Now, I can barely stand to wear my high heels when we go out to parties, and after one or two dances, my poor old bones are aching, and I begin to limp. And there's no point in dancing in tennis shoes. It just isn't dancing, not for a lady like me. I would rather limp!

My children told me to go ahead and get the surgery. My son the joker, he said, Mami, all you need is those bullet bands across your chest and a couple of pistols in holsters, and you'd look like a Mexican bandit; you are walking like you just got off the horse. He threatens to buy me a big cowboy hat if I don't agree to surgery. But I don't know. I don't feel right about it.

All my joints are worn, and I can't go around replacing everything. I've had a good, long life. Besides, what if I have the surgery, and all of a sudden I just die from the anesthesia? People do, and it's a very long procedure. Who would take care of my husband then? All we had were sons, and a daughter-in-law is not a daughter. I can't entrust my old man to someone who isn't a blood relative. So tell the doctor, thanks anyway, but I think I'll keep limping along with my old bones. Also, could you ask him if it's okay to wear heels just while we have company? I can't bear to have them see me in tennis shoes; they wouldn't understand.

7

Artificial Life

I'm glad to be in Seattle for medical care. I think if anyone can help me, they will be able to help me here. They have so much technology and so many doctors and all kinds of equipment that other people don't even know about. Like my mom, she had a bad burn, and they gave her something called Artificial Life, and she had a miraculous recovery. No one can believe it. But it's true; my mom recovered—I saw it with my own eyes! It happened like this.

My mother is very old, in her eighties, and she had a stroke, and she was mostly numb on one whole side, so she was in a wheelchair, and she was staying with my sister. And one day when my sister was doing some household chores in another room, my mother wheeled herself into the kitchen and grabbed the whole big pot of beans and tried to lift it off the stove, and it fell into her lap, and she was horribly burned.

My sister felt like death. She called the ambulance, and they flew Mom to Seattle in a helicopter all the way from Yakima, and none of us thought she would make it when we drove across the mountains. They wouldn't let anyone into the helicopter, not even my sister, and we had to drive the whole way not knowing what we would find. Could an old lady like our mother survive such a burn? It seemed impossible. But she did.

I don't know what all they did to my mother at that burn unit, but I know they took patches of skin and moved them from here to there like it was nothing, and they gave her something called Artificial Life, and it's like they can revive dead people. I don't know how they do it, but it is just miraculous.

They had my mother stay and live in the hospital for several weeks, and they kept changing her skin and putting new bandages on her and fixing her up over and over, giving her new layers. She just kept feeling better and better the more they did to her. They just took skin from one place and put it on another, and that skin would just start growing there like it had been there all along. I don't know how they could make it stick. These are mysteries.

My mother is as good as new or even better, so spry and energetic. She's still in a wheelchair, but she is more alert than ever. She has a lot of scars, but still, she is fine, and she herself has said to many people that she was dead, she was really gone, and then they gave her Artificial Life. It's been several years, but I can't help but still admire those doctors, and I still wonder how they did something that before only God could do. I still can't believe we still get to see our mother every day, here on earth. It is truly amazing.

Auto Tech

I was going to become an auto technician here, but it's just too expensive. So I'm saving up to move back to Guadalajara and take the course there. Here, they were going to end up charging more than six thousand dollars, and in Mexico, it's going to be eighteen hundred for the whole course. The education system in the United States is so expensive and so crazy!

Think about this. They tell me to come on over to the community college, because they are only going to charge me seven hundred dollars a quarter for the auto-tech program. Next thing you know, they are saying that, by the way, you have to pay these extra fees to use the workshops and garages. You have to pay to use the tools. You have to sign up for a welding workshop or something, and they are going to charge you for that separately. Then you have to buy some other equipment that you thought was included, and you have to own it yourself and not use theirs.

That's bad enough, but that's not all. The academic advisor, she went down a list of things you have to take for auto tech. English 103, a bunch of other things, and Psychology 101. I told her, I said, wait a minute. What do you expect me to do, lay the driver down in the reclining driver's seat and psychoanalyze him while I fix his car? I'm not working on human minds here; I just want to fix engines, work on cars. Maximize performance and get things running. Not heal the psychic wound. I told her, I want to fix cars that squeak, not work on primal screams, you know, where you throw plates at the wall or something? I read about that in one of my mom's magazines once. Like a form of therapy. Why do I need to learn that? I mean, come on. I want to be a, what do you call it here, a grease monkey, that's all.

She tells me, sorry, but you will not be granted your auto-tech degree if you don't successfully complete Psychology 101 and all the other required courses, whether you agree or not. Psychology 101, can you believe it? To fix people's engines. Tell me they're not doing it just to cheat the students out of even more money. Because of course we have to pay extra for every single credit hour. The more they make us take, the more money they make.

So that's why I'm going to Mexico. I pay a single, onetime, eighteen hundred dollar fee, they provide supplies, they provide the cars to work on, they provide the tools, they show me how to fix engines, and I don't have to pay three times that much and study Freud to be an auto tech. Sure sounds like a deal to me. Hey! Maybe when I'm done, I'll move back here and work as a mechanic to pay my way through college and study psychology! Nah, just kidding.

Back

I've used my back to earn a living for thirty years, since I was eight years old. In Mexico, I would join my father in the fields and do whatever I could to help him out in his labor. He was a hardworking peasant, and he took the best care he could of all of us, but there was no way to have all of us go to school. It was too far away. He had to choose a few of the younger ones to get some schooling, and they didn't get much, either.

So when the doctor said he could put this steel box with holes in it in my back to replace the disc that was destroyed from all the years of overuse, I took him up on it. And I know he said it would still hurt after it was done, because other parts of my back are worn down as well, but it never crossed my mind that it might hurt worse than it did before surgery.

The doctor showed me my X-rays at the follow-up appointment, and it looked to me like that little steel box was in crooked, but he says it isn't, it's just the angle of the picture as it was taken. I got up the nerve to ask the doctor, is there any chance it could be crooked, and you could go in and fix it? He said, number one, it's not crooked, and number two, you have a lot of scar tissue, since you had a major surgery, and going back in there would only make things worse.

That's when he sent me to you, doctor, to go through your pain clinic and rehabilitation program. And I've done all those exercises to the best of my ability. I've learned all about the proper body mechanics and lifting techniques and how to protect your back at work. And you had said you hoped the leg pain was muscular and not nerve, since that is easy to fix with exercise. And I've done the best I can to get better, but I still hurt. And you know I just can't lift anymore, not like I did before. And now there isn't any more treatment left to get.

I have to say, I'm surprised that Labor and Industries insurance doesn't have to help me do my old job; they only have to get me so I can do any job at all. I was earning fifteen dollars an hour, but now they think I could get a job for minimum wage, so they can cut off my benefits. And the only retraining they have to give me is up to six months. But doctor, I never had a chance to go to school. How can I learn to read and write, and learn English, and learn a trade, all in six months? This is the first schooling I've been offered in my life, you understand?

Doctor, thanks for the Kleenex. I'm sorry to be crying into my hands like this. In front of you and in front of the interpreter. But I've always earned my living with my back. I'm a young man. With my back gone, what am I supposed to do for the rest of my life? I'm scared, and I don't know where to turn. How am I going to live?

Beatings

They don't know how I got this cancer. They are going to operate now and take out what they can, and then I will have to get more treatment. Maybe radiation, and chemotherapy, and they said I might even need more surgery after this one. They can't tell me what all I will have to go through until after this surgery, I guess. And they can't tell me how or why I got this cancer, either. Everyone has their own ideas about that, I guess.

I know you heard my mom mutter something about beatings. What she means is this. She thinks he made it happen. Now, you've met my husband, and you know he's a kind man, but drink makes him crazy. He was never a rough or vulgar man, believe me. We are both peasants, but that doesn't mean we're all brutes, like they say. Not at all. He's a gentle man.

He was fine for the first few years. Never drank, worked hard, upright and decent. Came straight home from work. That was in Mexico and California. Then the work dried up, and we had to move up here to Washington. I don't know what changed, but he got bitter. He got unhappy and angry all at the same time. He took to drinking, and he got mean, even to me.

The first time it happened, I couldn't believe it, and neither could he. He just struck out at me, like I was a man. He knocked me down, then he wanted to help me up. I was so shocked, I didn't say a word. I didn't look at him or speak to him for three days, and he apologized all over himself. He was so ashamed and hurt, and he loathed himself for his own weakness. Since then, he has tried to quit drinking, but every time he gets laid off, or the work ends due to weather, or the rent is due and we just don't have it all, some of that rent money, it goes to beer.

My mom has begged me to leave him, but in Mexico, we have a law that the father always gets the kids. He told me that if I leave, he will take the kids to Mexico, and I'll never see them again. Then he would be beating them instead of me, and how does that help anyone? Besides, I know in my heart he doesn't want to hurt me. He's like a child having a tantrum, and he strikes me out of his own frustration and rage. It's not me. It's not him. It's just everything, the whole situation. It's nobody's fault, but still I wish I could fix it and make it right.

I wish I could make this country right for him or make Mexico right for him so he could support his family there. It's not that he doesn't want to work hard; he is a hard worker. But he needs a place where there's steady work and he gets paid regularly. Then he could be a man without hitting me. I truly pity him from my soul. That's why I won't leave him, no matter what Mom says. I just keep praying he will get strong and quit drinking for good. Maybe now…

Bible

What do you think about the second coming of Christ? Because He is coming, you know, and soon. He's coming any minute. You want to know how I know? I read the Holy Bible. That's God's message to His people. It's all in there. My wife and I are part of a small Christian community. It's our obligation to know what the Bible says and what it means. We think all good Christians should read the Bible every day.

This hasn't been easy for me. You know, a lot of people like me don't have a lot of education. It's hard to read the Bible, even in Spanish. I struggle a lot. I find myself falling asleep over the Bible, but then I know it's the devil at work. The devil, oh boy, he wants me to fall asleep, doesn't he? He and his evil ways! He wants us to fall asleep while we're reading the Holy Scriptures, or drift off and start thinking about something else, or not understand.

But that's when our faith takes over, you see. People with a lot of doubts, they might say, oh, I'm tired. I'm hungry. I want to work a second job and have more money to spend. Those doubters, they aren't going to be reading the Bible as much as I am. They are letting the devil whisper in their ear and tell them what to do, to be less faithful to God.

Me, I force myself to keep reading for two hours every evening. And when I get tired and start to fall asleep, I get to my knees, and I pray to God for the energy and the strength to keep going. I imagine there are seven devils trying to pull me away, and I sit up straighter, and I stare at the written page until it starts to make sense to me again. I learn a lot that way.

That's why I ask you, what do you think about the second coming of Christ? Because He is coming, and all the signs are in Revelations, there for anyone to read. The signs are taking place out in our society and around the world as we speak. It is that real. That's why we have to get ready, and the only way to get ready is to read the Bible, over and over.

It's not easy to keep reading the Bible; so much of it is hard to understand, but I know in my heart that people like me, who try and stay humble in relation to our Lord, who try to do His will and keep to His laws and read His book, we will be saved. We will see heaven. We will enjoy eternal life at the foot of His throne. And I know in my heart that the Holy Bible is taking me to heaven, word by word. *In the beginning was the word, and the word was with God, and the Word was God.* That's in the Gospel according to John. And that tells us that reading the Bible is like listening directly to God. How could He not love us for that? I feel sure, I have faith, that he loves us in our struggles. Praise the Lord!

Big

Yes, I'm big for a Salvadoran. I mean, I'm five feet nine inches and a hundred and seventy pounds. That's big for a woman, and I do stand out. I have had a lot of men tell me they find me attractive. No, I didn't know that short man who turned and followed us to the elevator. You think he was following me because he thinks I'm beautiful? Oh, ha ha! I don't know about that. I mean, maybe he was just lost.

When Latinos are lost somewhere, they will look around for another Latino. Then they will approach them and ask them in Spanish, like, do you know how to find such-and-such a place? Do you know what bus would take me to Issaquah? Do you know which hospital is Harborview? And they will look for another Latino because they think then they have a friend, someone they can speak Spanish to, who can help them more readily.

Oh, come on, you're just teasing me. I'll bet that guy was just going to ask me for directions or something. Ha ha. You think he might have been gathering up his courage to come into the elevator with us? Then why did you scare him off? You almost shut the door in his face, and you were pointing him out to me. Poor thing. Ha ha. Maybe he was just lost.

Well, you never know. When Latinos see a woman that pleases them, they might very well follow her for a little ways, and then try and talk to her and let her know how they feel, that they are interested. They might try to just strike up a conversation and try their luck that way.

In El Salvador, people have such a strict and regular routine. A man might follow you for weeks or even months, and you will never say a word back. You just completely ignore him, and he will walk alongside you every time you go to get tortillas at 4:30 p.m., and he'll keep asking you, like, what's your name? Why are you so shy? Why won't you talk to me? Don't you want to give me a chance? And you, as the woman, have the luxury of ignoring him for the longest time, to test his seriousness and see if he is really interested.

But here, see, if a Latino approaches me and shows his interest, and I just ignore him, chances are I'll never see him again. There are what, a million, two million people in the city? And we don't have a regular routine where we are always in the same place at the same time. So we Latinas have to get a little brave and say something right away. We have to take a lot more risk here. So why did you scare the poor little man off the elevator? I could have handled him. I'm used to short men, you know! Ha ha, you've ruined my chances, but then maybe he was just lost. Or maybe I reminded him of his long-lost mother. That's why they like us big, you know.

Book

S ometimes I wonder why we couldn't make it. If only people could know how many hopes and dreams I had when I came to this country two years ago. I sold everything we owned—our house, our furniture, even most of our clothes—to join my husband a few months after he came here. I believed that story that if you work hard, you can get ahead. I was filled with a desire to give this country the best that was in me, but I only found closed doors and nowhere to turn. So here we were, with three children and all these dreams, but no steady work.

We never got ahead. The jobs kept drying up on us. Or my husband would do yard work for a week and then get laid off. Or he would be asked to work for less pay or just not get paid. Or we would get hired in a fast-food restaurant, and then they would check our ID and fire us without giving us our paycheck. And we had to pay $800 a month to live in an unheated basement with just two mattresses to share for the five of us. And we couldn't get any help, since we are undocumented. The only help we could get was helping ourselves, and we wanted to work, but the work kept drying up, so we decided to move to Florida.

My husband heard through a friend there was a good, steady job in Orlando, so we drove our old car there and then it broke down, but we didn't care; we were so happy to have a chance for steady work. But it was a lie. There was no work; the jobs were taken while we drove there, and now we had no jobs, no money, and no way back. In the movies, this is where some nice person finds you and helps you, and you end up running a restaurant or something, but that didn't happen. We were on the street with nothing and no one to reach out a hand to us.

I called my only friend here, and she agreed to pay for our train ticket back to Seattle; that was the cheapest way we could find to travel. But in Montana, the INS agents boarded the train and took us off and held us for six hours and interrogated us and wrote us up a voluntary deportation order, but that means we have to save up for our own plane tickets for our one-way trip home within a couple months now. If we can't get the money together, we will be forcibly deported, and then there is a lifetime ban and jail time for reentry, even for the children.

So this is one story that didn't turn out like they say, and I am seriously thinking about writing a book about our experiences. People think low wages and high prices are a Latin thing, but no. Life has been horrible here. I have aged a lifetime in the last two years, and I suffer from nightmares and so much anxiety. My son cries whenever he sees a police now, and I would like to write a book and tell my people, don't come. It isn't like the movies. Don't come.

Braces

My son and I both have braces on. We got them because we had insurance through my husband's job. He has his papers, you see, and he learned English, so he had a steady job, and he worked there for fifteen years. Then they got a new manager, and that manager just told him, you have to go. No reason; just, we are changing things around, and you have to go.

So all of a sudden, my husband doesn't have a job after fifteen years in the same place. And me and my son, we are in the middle of having braces, and now our orthodontist said sorry, but since you don't have insurance, you have to pay a bunch of cash, or I can't keep treating you. I can't afford to just take small payments, he told us. I have to make a living.

My son has been in treatment for three years and has two years to go. He needed an expander and then teeth pulled and now braces. I just needed braces. I've had them on for a year and have about a year left. We have paid several thousand already, maybe two thousand on mine, and four thousand on my son's braces, and the insurance has paid that much again, but the orthodontist said it's not enough. He said he needs more than a thousand cash deposit before he can do any more adjustments. He said he can't take the braces off for free, either. He said he's sorry, but he just can't afford to do that. He wouldn't make any money that way.

So I got us signed up for medical coupons through the Department of Social and Health Services. We are low-enough income, and we have the right immigration papers. And I called all the orthodontists in the area. But not a single one of them will take medical coupons. So I called the medical-coupon number; they have a toll-free number. And they told me that they don't pay for braces unless you have a really bad cleft palate; they said it's like breast implants, just for looks. They don't think it's important. But we already have the braces on, so what do we do?

I called all the free and low-cost dental clinics in the area. But none of them have orthodontists; they just do fillings, and we don't need any fillings. They said orthodontia is not a priority. So I called the dental school, and they have an answering machine that says they can't take any messages and they can't make any appointments and they can't call anyone back or answer questions, and if we still have questions, we should call back next month. I guess they are just too busy with all the other poor people around, now that the economy is so bad.

So my question is, can you help us find someone, anyone, who will take our braces off for us, before our tooth enamel goes bad? Do you think anyone would help us if we make payments? It might take us a while, but we promise to pay it all. We're honest people.

Breast

Doctor, I know you want to check my baby since he was just born, but I beg you, I implore you, I pray to you, with all my heart, do not keep my baby away from me. I need to have the baby on the breast. You can observe him here, on my breast. I must have my baby with me. I beg you in God's name, do not take my baby. I need my baby with me.

I know, I know he had trouble breathing, but that's only because you startled him. You grabbed him straight from the womb, and you took him away from me to that cold table. No, I don't care if it's heated; that's not what I mean. I have to hold him. I promise you he will feel fine if you just please, please, put him on my breast, here. Of course you can take him if he isn't breathing well, but he's going to breathe easier at the breast! Please, let me have him now! I know I'm still getting stitched up; I don't care! Do you want me to walk across the room to that table, the needle and thread hanging from my womb? I must have my baby.

I can't believe you are asking for a reason! I thought you were a doctor who did deliveries all day long! Okay, doctor, I'll tell you why it's so important to me. It is imperative that I hold the baby right away. I have to bless the baby. I have to do rituals over the baby. I have to tell the baby his secret name and his public name. I have to tell the baby who he is, and to orient him to this world. I have to present the baby to myself, his mother, and tell him who his ancestors are. I have to touch the baby and love the baby. And I have to hold him to the breast, even if for a short while. There are a multitude of blessings and instructions that have to happen now. Please, young doctor. In case you ever become a father, do this for me now.

There! There you are, oh, my dear, beloved son! Oh, thank God! Finally! Oh, my dear, beloved child! Well, I am your mother! I can see you recognize me, and I recognize you. You belong to me, and to your father. Let me stroke you, let me touch you. Aren't you so perfect? Didn't you just come here to stay? Aren't you the healthiest and nicest little baby to ever travel under my heart? Thank you so much for coming to me, of all people, when you are such a desirable and beloved baby. Welcome to this life, beloved friend of mine, my precious treasure.

You don't need to be afraid anymore. I know the doctor startled you. Now that you are on the breast, you know where you belong, and you have nothing to fear. I have some instructions for you that you mustn't forget. Come, come closer, and listen to my words. These are private matters, between mother and son. You can close your eyes if you want, as long as you keep listening. Oh, and interpreter, thank the doctor and tell him to please stand back.

Bro

C ome on, sister-in-law! You can do it. Just keep on working! Give it all you've got! This baby's on his way out, any minute now! You heard the nurses. Push, honey, push! Keep it coming! Now rest. Hey, brother, get her a washcloth. Get her hair out of her eyes. Make sure she's comfortable and ready to push. Go on, Bro. Keep Sissie happy; she's having your baby!

Do you want anything? Do you want a sip of water? You're not scared, are you? You have nothing to be scared about. You're doing great, sister-in-law. The doctors said it's going to come out any minute. The baby's going to be fine. He's on his way out.

You see that paper there? That's the heart monitor. They can see the baby's fine. The heart is beating strong and steady; nothing wrong with this child. He's an eager, willing creature, just coming out to meet us now. So don't be afraid to push too hard; you can't hurt him. He's fine. He's a strong little one, and perfectly healthy. So buck up, take courage, and let's push him out, then. Give it all you've got!

There we go, good job, good job, sister-in-law! Looking good, looking good! Here he comes, by God! Here comes my nephew. That's right. Keep it up, don't slow down, sister-in-law! Another deep breath and hold it and push! Push with all your strength. We're seeing some hair now! His little head is under the bone, on his way now. Any push could be the last one.

Keep it up, keep going, sister-in-law. Give it everything you've got! Don't give up. Take her hand, brother, hold her hand. Support her neck so she can concentrate on pushing. Make sure and wipe her face between contractions; she's getting hot now. Keep her comfortable so she can push better. Come on, you two, now, work together. That's right.

Here it comes, by God! There's the head. Bravo, sister-in-law, here comes your baby! He's healthy! Here comes the body. Yes, it's a baby boy. That's right! Good job, sister-in-law. He's out now, his eyes are open. He's breathing just fine. Can you see him, sister-in-law? Look down, look down at him, sister-in-law! Bravo! Bravo, sister-in-law! Hurray!

Come, can we leave them alone for a minute now? Can we go in the hall?

You thought it was strange, didn't you, that I was so eager to cheer on my sister-in-law. But there's a part of the story you didn't know. She and my brother lost their first baby; he died at birth. And then they split up and didn't live together. It took me two years to get them back together. But I couldn't let my brother give up a woman like my sister-in-law just because they lost a baby, when they have their whole lives ahead of them. I had to help him. He's my bro.

Brother

My husband had to fly to Honduras for a month because his mother is ill, but he didn't want me to be alone, you see, in case I get sick or need help with anything. So he told his brother to move in with me until he got back. His brother is very nice, and he is very obliging. He wants to do everything to make sure I am well cared for, and he's very kind.

With this doctor's appointment, he had to work at the time I needed a ride. I told him, don't worry about it. I can take the bus downtown. He said no way. He said, I told my brother I was going to take care of you, and I'm going to take care of you. What if you took the bus and something happened to you? My brother would never forgive me! You are under my care now! I'll get you to your appointment, he said.

So his brother found a friend to drop me off. And the friend told me, here is my cell phone number. You just call me up when your appointment is over, and I will come right over and give you a ride home. Don't be embarrassed; just go ahead and call me, he said. I owe the brother a favor anyway, so I don't mind one bit. Really!

So that's how it is in my husband's absence. I have someone to give me rides and arrange for help. He is also taking my kids around where they need to go when I have to work. He is helping with food also, since he says he didn't come to be a burden, but to help us out. And he also works full time, so this is a lot for him to do for us, I think.

But my husband said, you have to understand Hondurans. They are not just going to leave their poor wife all alone for a whole month. They take all their obligations seriously. Family is everything, he told me. If I can't be there myself, I'm going to make sure someone I trust completely can be there in my place, and that is my brother.

Gee, I teased him. What if your younger brother takes too much care of me? Maybe I will start to prefer him if he is very attentive and really watches out to see how he can please me and keep me happy. That goes a long way with a woman, I told him.

That's the point of having it be my brother and not just one of my friends, he told me. I'm not stupid. He could no more be with you than be with our own sister, because you are his sister now, he told me. Gee, I told him. I never knew you were protecting yourself as well.

But really, even though I tease my husband for making all these arrangements for me, I like the attention. He really does take good care of me, and so does his brother. They're good men, my husband and his brother are. Even if they are Hondurans and not Mexicans, ha ha.

Bullet

Yes, I got her pregnant, but I didn't marry her. You have to understand how things were at the ranch. Now, a ranch isn't what white people seem to think it is. It's not a huge farm with cattle and all that. That's a myth. A ranch, now, that's a place so small you can't rightly call it a village. It has at most twenty or twenty-five families, almost all related one way or another. No police, no mayor or anything, just us. We make all the rules. It's been sixty years, but I don't suppose it's changed all that much. Things change slowly in the smaller places.

We all packed guns, the menfolk, that is. We had to, to take care of the animals and protect ourselves from robbers. It's a lonely area, a ranch. I knew how to use a gun already when I was a boy. When I was fifteen, I already had my own horse and rode out to do my own work. My father lived with his real wife, so I did the main bulk of the work on my mom's little section. Because I was able to travel, I could get with the ladies, if you know what I mean. Don't mean to be crude or offend you in any way, but you get my drift, I think.

Some girls were shameless and would offer themselves to me in exchange for nothing, not even a promise. Some for pay. Most of the girls would just push me off and tell me, if you're all that interested, you can go talk to my dad about it. But I was a young buck, fifteen, sixteen years old, with a handsome face like my father's and a long life ahead of me. I wasn't in the market for marriage. Then there was the one girl, Luz; I thought she was a good girl, too.

She wasn't one of the ones you can go to, for money. She had never been with a man, but she gave me liberties, one after another. She met me alone without permission, and she let me touch her all over. She took pleasure from me, and she let me take her maidenhead. She gave me her virginity, and she still wanted to see me. She was just crazy about me.

When I came onto her ranch later, she told me she was pregnant. She told me we had to get married. I told her, look, I didn't force you. I didn't hold a gun to your head. You know I can't marry you, because I would be a laughingstock. Everyone would say I married a whore. The fact that you're my whore doesn't change anything. You know I have to marry a virgin.

Long story short, she said she understood. We were together again a later evening, and she asked to see my gun, just to hold it. She aimed it at my head and said, is this how it works? And she shot me. That's how I got the bullet lodged in my brain, sixty years ago. Doctors say if it moves, I'm a goner. But it's been there for so long now, I'm kind of used to it. Besides, we all have to die sometime. Maybe I had sixty more years than I should have.

Calendar Boy

My son, he has disappointed his mother. We expected him to go to college and become an architect. He was interested in that before, but not anymore. He says he can make more money modeling, and believe it or not, he has become a calendar boy. Nothing indecent; he wears swimming trunks. But hardly a profession his mother can brag about to her friends.

We moved to this country when he was a young teen, and I know it was hard for him to adjust. He used to tell us, it's all going to be worth it because I'm going to become an architect and make lots of money. He was so good at math and drawing, and he seemed like a natural for architecture. He always had a strong sense of space, and beauty. His mother was especially proud, since her father was an architect. She was happy to have him follow her family tradition.

Well, he started taking a photography class in his last year of high school, and the teacher arranged for them to take glamour shots of each other and then sent the photos to a modeling school, and next thing you know, my son was getting offers to model! He did some ads, like clothing companies and some other products. Nothing indecent or anything like that.

He's a sharp boy, my son. Because he's so smart, he didn't really like other people telling him how to pose and what to wear and how to look. He had an idea of how he wanted to appear on camera, and he didn't like being told how to present himself. He's a very proud young man, a little like his old father maybe, ha ha.

So he got some backers to do the marketing and launched his own modeling company. They put together calendars of his photos; photos of him on the beach, or doing sports, or just looking into the camera as if he were having a candlelit dinner with you, and you can imagine you are his date. Nothing indecent, but pretty mm-mm-mm, if you know what I mean. And he sells posters and cards and calendars and even magnets, I think.

So now he's twenty-five, and he swears he's not going to go to college, because he's making more money now than he could make as an architect, so why go to college? He gets up at noon and stays up half the night, and he still looks good. My wife is not happy about it, but what can you do? He's a young man, he likes to have his fun, and he's driving a very nice car. Hard to tell him to run along and become a college freshman when he's raking in the dough.

He's a beautiful young man; that's how he can sell so much. A lot of people want to hang him up on their wall and look at him. How did he get so beautiful? Well, I have been called handsome in my day, but no, no, he takes after his mother in looks, ha ha!

Chains

I know he doesn't mean any harm, but the doctor hurt my feelings when I told him I was lonely and he suggested I could meet someone at the bus stop. I can only imagine that as a successful professional, he doesn't have many occasions to take the bus, otherwise he would know that most of the Latino men at the downtown bus stop where I transfer are alcoholics and street people with mental health problems. Is that what he thinks of me? I hope not.

The doctor is very nice, and he doesn't wear a wedding ring. He is the kind of man I would like to meet. I wish he could recognize that I am also an educated person, even if my English is not yet perfect. After all, I was a prosecuting attorney in South America. I only moved here due to the economic crisis. But the doctor appears to think all Latinos are Mexicans, and all of us are poor and uneducated. That's so misguided.

I am not allowed to practice law in the United States. I cannot even work as a paralegal, since I don't speak enough English yet. That is why I am working as a nanny. Can you imagine? I earn more money, with the devalued exchange rate, by changing diapers and feeding two babies than I earned as a prosecuting attorney at home. I can keep my son in college, but only by leaving my country and changing diapers for a living, not by practicing law. Something is horribly wrong with the world economy when this can be true.

It is incredibly lonely here. I have heard there are many, many Latin professionals who moved to the United States, but I feel like I'm the only one in Seattle. I just don't know how to find people. Working as a nanny, I meet no one at all. My apartment building doesn't have any Latino men. And the men I meet at church or in the streets, it would raise the hair on your arms! I don't consider myself a snob, but I feel strongly that chains belong on pets, mainly dogs, not on men. I have met many men who think I would be impressed by their hairy chests, open-necked shirts, and four or five gold chains. But all I can think of is putting them on a leash and taking them for a walk.

When this rich couple interviewed me, they never asked about my education. They don't even know I'm a lawyer. They think I'm from Mexico, too. They asked me things that were beyond humiliating, like would I know to wash my hands after changing diapers and before preparing food. I stayed cheerful, but the tears poured down my face when I left the house. I wish people could see me, and know who I am. I am so alone, I feel like I'm disappearing.

Charity Care

T his social worker, this really nice one, she told us today that since my wife has cancer, we can get something called Charity Care. She said if we have any questions, we could call her later. She said there is a law about that, and it says that any hospital that accepts federal funds is supposed to help people for cheap or free if they can't afford to pay for their medical bills.

You fill out these papers, and they figure out if you make less money than this certain amount that the federal government says is poor enough to need help. Then you show some pay stubs from all your jobs, your rent and utility bills, the social security numbers for your legal children, and a bunch of other papers. It's a program for people whose jobs won't insure them.

The scary part is they make you apply for welfare at the welfare office, even though the law has changed and they won't give us any help, since we are not citizens. But the law says the hospital only has to give you Charity Care if you apply for government help and the government won't give you the help. That is when the hospital kicks in and is supposed to help you with the money the federal government gives them. So we are going to have to go to that welfare office and ask for something we know they won't give us and get a letter saying they turned us down.

The social worker, she said the welfare office won't call Immigration, but things are changing now, and it's hard to know what is going to happen. A lot of people are getting arrested and deported, and there are more workplace raids, and some people are being laid off or fired even from our fast-food or hotel-maid jobs, since now some of the white people want those jobs after they lost their better jobs, so things are getting really tough now, especially for us.

Anyway, we have to do all these things, and we have to keep trying because now my wife has cancer, and they said the treatment is going to be thousands of dollars, and I earn a thousand a month working full time, but no insurance, and now my wife can't work. I work a second part-time job, but we have so many bills. And I have to be around to take care of my wife, too.

I was wondering if you could help us talk to that social worker and ask if the hospital could take our bills from my wife's prior treatment at this hospital out of collections and put them into Charity Care. See, my wife has been sick for awhile, and we couldn't keep up with the bills. We were making payments, but they said it wasn't enough. I wish we would have heard about this Charity Care program before. Maybe we could have applied for it before things got so bad, and my wife could have had treatment earlier, but you know what? We are really grateful for the Charity Care program and glad to have a chance to be on it now.

Cholo

One of my granddaughters, she was diagnosed with arthritis when she was still young. They say it comes from the family, but that's hard to believe, since we are her family, and none of us have it. Some farmworkers say it comes from the chemicals, the ones we have to use at our jobs. But she never worked in the fields; her parents kept her in school. Anyway, the doctor told her she won't be able to have children or anything, since she is so sick. And she missed a lot of school, too. It was hard for her to make friends when she was absent a lot, except for this cholo.

This one boy, he dressed like a cholo, you know? The baggy pants and kind of gang stuff. Anyway, she told us he would carry her from class to class when her pain was bad, so she wouldn't have to walk. We were going to talk to him, since we didn't like that, but instead he came to talk with us. He told us he loved her and wanted to marry her and take care of her. And them just two little high school children! What would they know? Her mother, my daughter, she said, no, my girl is sick, who's going to give her a mother's care? Leave her to me.

Well, this cholo dresser, he didn't leave it alone. He still hung around our girl at school, still carried her, still walked her home. So we sat down with him again, and this time we brought two uncles who are police. They told him, we can't have a cholo in the family; we would be the laughingstock of the police department. You need to leave her be. And the boy, he said, I can take her in the bad way, or in the good way, and I want to do it right, asking for her hand and marrying her. I don't want to run away with a girl like so many others do, because I respect her and you. I don't want to do anything behind your back. I'm not a cholo, and I love her.

Well, over time, this cholo-dressing boy, he kept after her until the family relented, and he finally sat down with the family, and they said, you want her, you take her, but you have to understand: family is family, you can't back out of this one later. You take her, it's for life, knowing about her disease. If you later decide you want kids or something, and you try to leave her, you will have to answer to me. And me. And me. And me, each one of us said, all the way down the line, including my two police sons. And the boy said he accepted.

So my granddaughter, even though she is so sick and probably can't have any kids and may not live that long, she had this chance for happiness and she took it, and now it's been seven years, and you can believe it or not, just as you will, but they are like lovebirds, and they are together to this day. And he still dresses kind of like a cholo, but he never was a cholo; we just thought he was because of the way he dresses. You know? He just dresses kind of funny.

Choose

I was with this man from work for around a year, when I found out he actually had a family in Mexico. Of course, I was furious and broke it off right away, but old habits die hard, and after all, his family wasn't here yet. So we ended up fighting and getting back together and fighting and getting back together. And then his family showed up, in the form of a wife and two more kids, besides the daughter who already lived with him when he was with me.

Well, he and I still worked together, and I was buying his brother's car, and he was going to help me with something, changing the tires or something, and I had to go to his apartment building, just the parking lot, to deal with something about the car, and she came flying out the door like a devil on fire and just started screaming in my face in front of everyone. Loud.

Okay, well, I guess I should mention that I was still kind of seeing him from time to time, even though I know I shouldn't have. But you know, we were together for a long time, and it was more like I was his wife, his common-law wife, in Washington state, since we had lived together and I had taken care of him and his oldest girl who lived with him all that time.

So his wife was just saying things you wouldn't believe, and I finally told her, look, I said, you're just a Mexican wetback with no papers who can hardly even write your own name, and you might be his lawful wife in Mexico, but you're not in Mexico anymore, and you're nobody here. I have my papers, I told her, and I took your husband and your ungrateful bratty daughter in when they had nowhere to go, so why don't you ask her who let her stay with them for free and just go to high school and not even work; why don't you ask her that? And by the way, you are nobody here and all it would take is one phone call to Immigration and you can kiss your husband goodbye and head back to Mexico where you belong, so you'd better watch what you say, or I'll raise a scandal you will never live down!

Anyway, the husband came over and told us both to shut up, and I told him, you want us to shut up, why don't you be a man for once in your life and tell us both, to both our faces, right here and now, whom do you choose? Which one of us are you going to recognize as your wife? Because we are not going to just share you and have half a man each. And his wife said choose.

He surprised us both by saying neither one of you; I'm sick of both of you, and I'm sick of your fighting. Well, that was when I dumped him for good, because I could see he was never going to be serious about me. I only called him now because I'm so sick, and I thought he would want to know. If I were well, I never would have given him the time of day.

24

Church

We usually don't do this, but we have enjoyed talking with you so much that I feel called upon to share this with you. Here, let me find this in my purse. Ah, here it is. See this pamphlet? Yes, see, that is our church, and you are welcome to come. Jehovah's Witnesses? No, not at all, we're not Jehovah's Witnesses. We're not Catholic or any denomination. We are a faith-based Christian church. Just pure Christian. We follow the Bible, just as it's written.

My friend and I, we moved here with our families to be part of this Christian community. We go to church every Wednesday and Sunday for the big services, and then we have all kinds of services and prayer groups on other days. It is so sweet to sit in a group of other ladies and discuss Bible stories, or pray over the things we care a lot about, like the health of our children, how they are adjusting to school, keeping them close to God. Just whatever's on our mind.

We have singing and cheerful music. We are lively and fun. We dress up nicely for church, of course, but we are just comfortable and being ourselves. It isn't false or fake at all. A lot of people from all the races come to our services. The pastor and his wife are from Central America and were called to come here to Seattle and set up this bilingual church for our community, but a whole lot of other people come now, too. It is expanding. Growing.

The nicest thing about our church is the support. If someone is hurting, we help. If someone is ill, we lay our hands on them and pray, and we lighten their burdens. If someone is worried, we pray with them. If someone has lost a loved one, we give support and friendship and help console them in their sorrow. We are like a big family, you see, a family in God.

That's why we think you might like to join us. You say you have children, and our church is a very good place for children, to keep them on the path of righteousness. Aren't there ever so many snags and thorns along the path these days? So many traps and pitfalls, such as alcohol? Children can grow up so fast with television and movies and their schoolmates pushing them along. It's hard to keep them young and protected, unless you have a strong church, one that helps you keep Christ as your personal friend and Savior.

We know you might already be going somewhere. A lot of people don't like being asked to church. We aren't asking you to make you uncomfortable, but please come. At least come once. The only reason we asked you is because you are such a lovely person, and it is a very lovely church. We really think you'd like it. Please talk it over with your husband, and see if you can get him interested in joining our church. You won't regret it. God loves you.

Class

I am from South America. I'd rather not say which country, since I know you also work with my wife, and I don't want you to think less of her, but she is from the peasant class, and it's been very hard for me to be married to her. I think that's why I've been having so many health problems. I married her out of loneliness. I was so glad to find someone from my country in this small place; she was the first person I met from my part of the world, and I was so alone.

I saw right away that she was not educated, and I was secretly proud of myself for not judging her too harshly. I always thought class distinctions were ludicrous and that we are all the same and that given the chance for education, any person could rise above their station and become a better person, fit into any role. She was working as a hotel maid. And I daydreamed about educating her, helping her to see the world through a wider lens.

Both my parents, my whole family, are university educated. We are widely traveled, well read, have a good sense of what is going on in the world around us, are interested in music, art, and all play instruments. It is how we were raised, that these basic things are what make up a cultured, aware, and educated human being, someone who is capable of participating in life to the fullest, contributing to society. I speak adequate English at work; I just ask for a medical interpreter for these complex appointments, where my condition is being explained to me.

So I married my countrywoman here in the U.S., knowing she was someone I could never take home to Mother, but then, who can afford to travel? Life is short, and I was terribly lonely. I don't want to leave her because it's not her fault she's so limited. She was affectionate. She could cook the food I grew up with. She could speak to me in my language. She knew my culture, at some level. I tried to get her interested in English classes, other enrichments, but she frankly has no interest in education or expanding her views.

As time went on, she grew resentful of my attempts to help her. She started to swear more freely and show me the vulgar, crude person she truly is. She is self-satisfied and smug, and because she cannot understand what I am trying to offer her, she refuses it and mocks me. It is a daily agony for me to come home from work and find her sitting on the couch, watching Brazilian soap operas translated into Spanish, sometimes crying into a dishrag, while in the real world, a war is going on, there are uprisings in our homeland, and she couldn't care less. I married her of my own free will, and I will never leave her. But it is just so painful. I would never have married someone like her in my country. She might be my maid, but not my wife.

Classes

I had the hardest time with my little boy before, you wouldn't believe it. He wouldn't listen to anything I said, and I would have to repeat myself ten or twenty times to get his attention, and then I would have to yell at him and sometimes spank him, and sometimes I would get so frustrated I would just burst out crying and start screaming at him about why wouldn't he behave, and then I would hit him hard and then he would cry and I would cry so hard because I felt so sorry for him because after all, he's just a little boy, and I am supposed to be the grown-up.

Then my nurse told me I should take some parenting classes. I thought that was a little strange, to have classes for something that should be natural, but she said it's not. She said lots of people parent the way they were taught, but it isn't always the best way, and now they've done a lot of studies and you can take a class and watch films and read about all the things they now know will actually work with children, like positive reinforcement, they call it.

I went ahead and took the series of parenting classes. They taught us a whole bunch of things, but mostly, before each class, I would pray, God, please allow me to learn these techniques and become a better mother. I know now that it is not my little boy's fault that he makes me so crazy; it is my fault and I have to fix it, but God, could you look down upon me with mercy and notice I have a hard time with my child, and now you gave me this unexpected pregnancy and please help me, please help me to be strong and not frustrated.

I think God listened because I found the strength to follow the lessons and do the things at home, even some things I didn't think would work, and really, within just a few weeks, I started to notice that my son's behavior was changing, and he was listening to me and being more obedient, and that taught me that it really was me, that he could behave if I raised him right. So that made it easier to keep learning more about it and keep trying to use all those lessons in the home. A lot of people have noticed that he is behaving better than before.

Now that I know how to be a better mother and this unexpected pregnancy came along, I am praying to God a lot to give me patience, give me strength, don't let me fall back down, don't let me fall back into yelling at my little boy, don't let me punish my boy for my bad parenting. I think the classes I took are the only classes they have, so I have to make sure I can be a good enough mother with what I know now. Unfortunately for me, I don't have any family around to help me figure this out. That's why I just keep praying to God about it, and I hope He will be kind to me and my misbehaving son, and show us some compassion. And give me the strength.

Crossing

*I*t was when the doctors in Mexico were so rough on me that I decided to make the crossing. I had cancer in my woman's organs, and they just said, it's incurable. You are going to die. Just like that. No hope. I cried and cried and called my grown children in the U.S. and told them, I'm going soon. You'll have to come get your children and take them to the U.S. I can't care for them—I'm dying. And my oldest daughter, she said, no, Mom. We're not going to let you die. We'll all pay for your treatment in the U.S. All you have to do is get here.

So I set up the coyotes with borrowed money, and they were taking us across the border in separate groups, and I was so scared! Oh, my God I was scared! And I can't swim and they tied us together in groups and we had to walk across the river, but it was so brown and muddy and the water was moving and I just was terrified and they separated me from the children—I can't remember why—and then I got caught and deported, but the kids didn't. They made the crossing.

They told me later the coyote had to threaten to leave my 12-year-old grandson in the desert because he was going to get the whole group caught by crying out loud and saying, I want Grandma, I want Grandma. So it was very dangerous. Meanwhile, I was caught and deported, and then I had no choice but to cross again. And my family had to pay for both crossings. And I made the second crossing, thank God, but it was weeks of suffering and traveling, and I am sure my cancer got much worse and just grew and grew with all the stress. Horrible.

So I caught up with my grandchildren at my son's house in California, and they made the down payment for my surgery among the five working adult children, and the doctors removed my big tumor and said I was in delicate health and needed six weeks to recover before they could continue treatment. But then three days after my surgery, the landlord came and said we had too many people living there, and he was sorry I was ill but rules are rules and me and the grandkids that were not my son's children had to move out immediately, or he would evict us all.

That's how I ended up in Seattle now with my son, and that's why I had to switch my cancer treatment to this hospital. And I hope they won't charge us a lot more for having to switch hospitals, since the children are paying cash for everything and it is a lot of money and we wouldn't have come here except the Mexican doctors said I was going to die and the California landlord wouldn't let me stay there and now here I am and I hope I get cured so I can work and pay back some of these thousands to my children before I die. That is my goal. To work again.

Otherwise, none of this will be worth it: the crossing, the surgery, the radiation, the pain.

Daughter

I want a healthy baby, that most of all, but why deny it? I would also like a son. A daughter, I would love her, of course, but a son, well, I could take him everywhere with me. I would have him as my constant companion. You know girls are so attached to their mothers as a rule, and then they don't have time for old Dad. You probably were like that yourself, ma'am.

You weren't? You liked doing things with your Dad? Well, I guess it takes all kinds. Fishing, huh? And working at his shop? Well, I'll be. Playing cards with his friends? That would sure surprise my buddies to see a little girl doing that. That's pretty funny.

I wish we could have found out at the ultrasound if we were going to have a girl or a boy; that way we could be more prepared for it, you know. But I guess it wasn't God's will. I don't know why we Latinos want our firstborn to be a male; it only happens half the time, right? And it's not like we have a castle for them to inherit or anything, ha ha. It just seems like my wife has been pushing for hours now, and there just has to be a little boy in there trying to get out. Girls are so co-operative as a rule. Seems like a girl would have been born already.

What? You think a girl might not want to come out, might not feel welcome? Do you really think the babies can hear? Well, yes, I know they have ears and everything, but do you think they understand language? They might? I guess the baby has heard us talking for months now. You think she might? Gosh, I didn't mean to hurt anyone's feelings! I would love to have a girl; I just meant to say that if it's a boy, I would take him everywhere with me.

My wife has been pushing for so long now. It seems like it won't end. Do you really think? You do? Well, okay, I'll say it. And I'll mean it. Let me come right over the belly then, so the baby can hear me. Can you hear me, little one? This is your Daddy talking. Now listen, little one. Whether you're a boy or a girl. You are hurting your mother, so you'd better just come on out of there now. Come on out and meet us. It's time to face the light of day.

And listen, little one. If you are a boy, I'll take you with me everywhere. And if you are a girl, I'm going to love you just the same, and I'm going to take you everywhere with me, and it's okay with me if you are a little girl, because you'll be my daughter. In fact, I think it would be fun to have a little girl of my own to love and to cherish. Okay? I hope you can hear me, because I really mean it. So come on out now; your mother is pushing as hard as she can.

Oh, my God! I see the head starting to show! Honey, I bet it's going to be a girl! Look, honey, here comes our little daughter! May God bless her and keep her safe. Come to Daddy!

Dear Mami

Dear, Beloved Mami:

You just saw me die, so you know I can't write. I have asked someone to write this down for me, but I promise these words come from my heart, from the pure heart of your dead baby.

When God sent me to this world, he told me I would only have a little time. He told me all my time would be in the womb, and I would have to die there and come back to Him. So don't feel sorry for my sake; I knew all along that was all the time I had. I am not sad about it.

I am only sorry you had to suffer so much. I heard and saw everything you did for me, Mami, and I am eternally grateful. I saw you trying not to cry while you were in labor, even when the young anesthesiologist wouldn't give you an epidural because his book said not to give you pain medication until you get to a certain stage of labor. Forgive him, Mami. He never saw a dead baby before, and he was scared, too. He wasn't thinking about the fact that the risk of slowing down the birth couldn't harm me. I was already dead. He was scared, too.

I saw the nurse and the interpreter with tears in their eyes in the hall while they were trying to convince the new doctor to let you have pain medication. The interpreter told the doctor what you told her, that you were holding back your tears because you didn't want me to feel that I was hurting you. You wanted my last few moments on this earth to be pleasant ones and for me to enjoy them without suffering or feeling guilty, just in case I wasn't dead yet.

I know you suffered for me. I know you held back your tears for me. I love you so much for everything you have done for me. Maybe I can explain why I chose you, even though I couldn't stay long, and that will help you to think about me later with kindness, and no regrets.

Mami, it was already a given that I could not live outside the womb. So I asked God, could you grant me a mother whose heart is like an open door? Someone who can love me so much, even though I will just be in the womb. Even though I will not be perfect and I will not survive. And God was merciful and granted me that wish. Every day, as I grew inside of you, I knew you loved me. How glad you were to welcome me into this world, how sad at my passing.

I know this has been hard for you. But I hope you also understand, you were the best mother I could have ever hoped for, the best mother in the world for me. Thank you for loving me, thank you for carrying me under your heart all those months, thank you for all your mother's hopes and mother's wishes. My life was short, but I have no regrets. I know what it is to feel a mother's love, Mami, so thank you for that. I will never forget you and never stop loving you.

Death

I don't need the doctors to tell me that I nearly died. I felt it myself. I kept calling out—my husband said I was hallucinating, but it was real, it was real to me. "I'm going, I'm going, I'm going, I'm going!" I called out to him. "No, honey, you're right here, everything is okay," he answered me, but I couldn't hear him. I only found out about that later, when I came to.

To the left of me was the place they describe in the Bible—all the animals, the garden, beauty and peace, and no evil, only good. To the right of me, a dark graveyard. To the left, a spirit all in white. To the right, a spirit all in black, a long, black robe, no face to see. In front of me, two things: a dark hole, emptying into nothing, just emptiness. No light at the end of the tunnel, just darkness. Also, at times I saw a dark, wintry forest up ahead, just branches more than anything, filled with red lights, kind of like Christmas lights, except that they weren't really lights, and there was one white light, except it wasn't really a light. It was me; I was the white light, and all the red lights were evil spirits. I was alone, all alone and surrounded completely by evil spirits in a dark forest of despair.

At the same time—as I was lying in my bed and I could feel myself lying in my bed and swollen up with the pain and the infection and the fever and the bleeding, which wouldn't stop—I felt my whole upper body being lifted up in bed, but not by the nurses. I was being lifted and jerked and dragged toward the black cave, the empty hole, into nothingness.

I called out, "Leave me, leave me, leave me, leave me!" I called out, "Who are you, what are you? Are you evil or good?" The creature, this emissary of death, he didn't answer me; he just held me tighter around my upper body and he pulled, he pulled with all his might, and I was getting closer, closer to the cave, the cave of death. I was leaving everything I knew, but I wasn't going to heaven. There was no peace. It just felt cold, like a chill, cutting wind.

So I called out with all my might, "I am baptized. I am dedicated to the one and only God, Jehovah, and his Son, Jesus Christ our Savior, and no one else can touch me. No one else can own me. Only They own me. Only They have the power to decide my fate. If you are evil, leave me. Leave me, leave me, leave me! This I command you in the name of God the Father and Jesus Christ his Holy Son, the only true God and the only one who owns me body and soul."

Then I woke up in this bed, in the Intensive Care Unit, and my unborn baby was dead. God grant he had an easy journey to the other side, not being dragged and pulled by evil spirits like I was. May he rest in peace, the poor, innocent babe. I pray to God he saw the light.

Deer

My grandson, his mother left him with me in San Salvador while she went to the United States to work. She left when he was little, and he was alone with me for four years. We lived on the outskirts of San Salvador, and it was hard for me to try and raise him all alone. I did the best I could, and I tried to get him to mind, but there was a big gang of boys, all his buddies so to speak, who used to come to the door and try and get him to disobey me. They would say, don't listen to her, she's not even your mom, she's just your grandma, you don't have to mind her!

As long as I held eye contact with him, he would not leave, even though the gang of eight or ten boys would be in the doorway, goading him on to disobey me. But as soon as I turned around to do something else, I would turn back around, and he would be gone. Then I would tire myself out going from house to house, friend to friend, is my grandson here? Is my grandson here? They would all say no, and sometimes I would glimpse him hiding under a mango tree, and then he would dart off and run like a deer with his friends all around him, not looking back.

I finally called my daughter in Los Angeles and I told her, look, I know it's hard for you to have your child with you in the United States, but I can't handle him any more. He won't obey me. I'm no good to him any more. And imagine this: While I was thinking I couldn't handle being *with* him, he was thinking he couldn't handle being *without* me! The way it happened was this, my daughter came back to San Salvador to pick him up, and he refused to go!

He said he couldn't handle being without me! He absolutely refused to go with his own mother; he said he loved me too much! And when she tried to force him, well, you can guess what he did. He ran like a deer! Just like a deer! She couldn't catch him to save her life. She didn't know half his hiding spots, and she didn't even know his friends to make the rounds looking for him. I helped her all I could, but it was impossible. Finally, after a week of this, she said, Mom, could you consider leaving your country and coming with us, at least to settle us in?

Well, it wasn't so hard to decide. I could see what was going on in my neighborhood. A lot of boys were joining gangs and getting into trouble. In fact, most of the boys who were my grandson's inseparable companions are dead now. So instead of staying behind alone, I moved to Los Angeles and helped my grandson settle in. I ended up being with him until he was grown, and he turned out well. He is a respectful boy, and he loves me a lot, still. Now he is twenty, and I have moved up here to take care of my other daughter's children who are younger and need me more. But I miss my little deer, the runner.

Diabetes

I had to abort my first child because of diabetes. That was in my village. I didn't know I had diabetes, and by the time I found out, the doctors said there was too much damage to the baby. All the awful things that can happen to you from uncontrolled diabetes, they can happen to babies in the womb when the mother has diabetes. Because all this excess sugar is just coursing through your veins and getting into the fetus. And the baby gets damaged.

Believe me, it broke my heart to accept it. I didn't want to do it. But I didn't know anything, I was young and had no children, and they told me, the studies show this and this and this. The studies mean you are going to have a severely disabled child, and it will probably spontaneously abort, like a miscarriage, but then you will die, too. So we strongly recommend that you have an abortion for medical reasons. I was three months pregnant, and I aborted.

And then two years ago, I became pregnant again. But this time, they showed me everything. How to inject insulin. How to eat and what not to eat. How to measure food into servings. How to check my blood sugar. And they did all kinds of studies, even that one where they poke a long, long needle straight into your womb through the skin, and take amniotic fluid to the lab. Oh my God, that hurt! But they found that my child was perfect, and they explained that it was because my diabetes was controlled. It wasn't like the first time.

So now this time, I have even decided not to have the amniocentesis, because first of all, you have to take what God gives you. I didn't know enough the first time, I was so innocent. Now I have a child already, and I know the responsibilities of parenthood. In the second place, I am controlling my blood sugar with insulin, and I am already used to the whole procedure.

When I first had to poke myself, I just sat and cried. It isn't natural to poke or cut yourself, yet they wanted me to feel good about jamming a needle into my belly or thigh and poking my finger eight times a day. How could a normal, healthy person feel good about that? I didn't! I would cry and tell my husband, this is too hard, I can't do it, I can't go on.

For a while, he agreed to give me my shots, but then he would start to cry because I was crying, and he would feel sorry for me, and he would say let's just forget the shots—who will know? But then I had to be the responsible one and say, go ahead and inject me; it's hard but we have to accept this. It's the only way we're going to get a healthy baby, and that's what it's all about. Diabetes can't stop you from having kids, not if you know what you're doing. I'm having my third one now, well, my second living one, God willing. I know I'm doing my part.

Doctor

I'm sorry I ever went to the doctor. I just never felt worse than I do now that I've had this surgery. I feel worse than ever. I just wish I had never seen the doctor at all, to tell you the truth. I think doctors can't help but want to fix something once they see it; but what if the doctor had never seen it! Then he never would have wanted to fix it. So that part is my fault.

This was a problem I had for thirty years, since I had an accident in my youth. That's when the hernia came out, and it never bothered me. I worked all the years of my life with no problems. Physical labor. Farmwork. Hard work. Nobody ever said a word about it. I never asked for an opinion about it. And it all only came out because of my greed.

Instead of doing plain old farm labor like I always had, I decided I wanted a little more money. So I tried to get my commercial license so I could drive the farming equipment. Well, they make you take a physical for your commercial license. And in the physical, the doctor told me I had to have that hernia repaired to get the license.

Now I could have just not gotten the license, but I wanted to get more money. I wanted an easier job in my older years. I went and found a doctor who could do the surgery, and he said it was simple, and he did it. Then I went back to the doctor for the physical, and he said I need to get the hernia repaired. And I said, no doctor, I already did. And he said, look how it's bulging. You need to get it repaired again.

So I had to go back to the doctor and have it repaired again. It had ripped open again. And I don't know what the heck happened, but it didn't work the second time, either. So then they sent me to another doctor, the real expert, and he did a third surgery. And like I said to the surgeon here, I said, no offense, but I'm sorry I ever went to the doctor about this because I have more pain, more swelling, more scars, and more of everything bad since I went to the doctor in the first place. And now I can't work at all. I'm disabled!

The doctor just kind of laughed at me and said, you should have gone to the doctor a long time ago. But honestly, what for? So they could have done three surgeries on me back then, and I would have spent all those years unable to work, and I would have had who knows what complications from it by now? No. The truth is, I wish I had never gone to the doctor in the first place. Now I can't drive heavy equipment, and I can't do farmwork, either. I can't do anything.

If a doctor can't fix you, he should just leave you alone. But you know a doctor can't stand to see something without trying to fix it. That's the problem with doctors. No offense.

Dog

"The lone dog may lick himself, but the married dog is not allowed to," as the saying goes. That's what my husband used to tell me when we were first married, and now I've been repeating it to my daughter-in-law, even though she doesn't seem to understand. Have you heard that saying before? It's a common one.

You know how dogs like to, well, lick their private parts? Just be relaxed and do as they feel without really noticing how it looks to anyone else? Well, if a dog is accompanied, or married, the female dog will act like, what do you think you're doing, all spread out there and licking yourself? Don't you realize how ridiculous you look? Cut that out; it's gross! Then the male dog feels embarrassed and uncomfortable, like he can't just be himself. He can no longer relax because he's always getting in trouble, getting scolded and bossed.

A lot of new brides do the same thing to their human mates. They are constantly telling them, pick up your dirty clothes. Why did you leave that dish in the sink? You have soup on your moustache. Do you have to fart in the kitchen? Can't you go somewhere else to do that? Why are you watching television with your hands on your crotch? What's wrong with you?

The poor husbands, they don't mean any harm. They are just trying to feel at home in their homes. My son, when he lived with me, I didn't badger him. I didn't badger his father. If I saw my son wearing a dirty T-shirt, I didn't follow him around telling him he looked awful and making him change. I figured he knew what he was doing. He was comfortable and happy.

But my daughter-in-law, she says her mother told her to lay down the law from day one. Her mother warned her, whatever you can get your husband to do, do it now while the marriage is still fresh, because you'll never get him to change later. This is your only chance. If you let him throw his clothes down now, he'll never pick them up. If you scrub and clean and serve him, he'll never get off his butt. Whatever you do now, you'll be stuck doing until the day you die. So you have to lay down the law from the get-go, her mother told her.

I see her point in a certain, small way. I mean, it's hard to suddenly ask a man, like my husband, to get up and make his own breakfast. He's used to me doing it. But our men work hard, especially living in this country. They don't feel like a big man in their jobs. They don't earn as much as a lot of other men. They don't drive nice cars or have lots of nice clothes. They can't buy us the kinds of houses that people on the soap operas live in. So why not let them play the big man at home? Why not remember that "the lone dog may lick himself"? What harm is it?

Donors

I don't want to sound overly proud, doctor, but I just want to let you know up front: I will not be needing to be on the wait list for a kidney transplant. I have plenty of donors. More than enough of them, to tell you the truth. I must still be a pretty useful old woman, because a lot of my relatives want to keep me around. The longer the better, from what they say.

I have three sons, all grown, and every single one of them wants to donate a kidney. They already agreed; whoever has the kidney that is the best match, he will be the one. That way, it's fair between the three of them. If for some reason, none of them can be the donor, then my daughter said she would. She just doesn't want to be first on the list amongst the children, since she has young children of her own to take care of. So she's fourth in line.

Even my eleven-year-old granddaughter, the oldest of my grandchildren, she said she's not going to lose her grandma just because of a silly old kidney, and she told her mother she wants to be a donor, but the doctor said she's too young. Still, I won't be needing a kidney from a stranger, God willing. And you already know who my first choice is, if you could see past his age: it's this man right here beside me, my dearly beloved life companion and husband.

We've been together since I was fifteen and he was twenty-eight, and that was forty-five years ago. I know him like the palm of my hand, and I think his kidney would suit me just fine. Now, I know he isn't the youngest of men, but doctor, he's like one of those old cars that someone took care of with loving care over many years that runs like new. My husband, he's had that care from me, you understand? He's never drunk alcohol or smoked in all the days of our marriage, and he doesn't have diabetes or any of those diseases that can age your kidneys before their time. So he's really like a much younger man.

Ever since I was just a girl myself, not much older than my granddaughter, he has been so attached to me. I think his kidney would take very easily and just be a natural part of me really well. He's already said he's going to stay with me the whole time, for the procedure and everything, never leaving my side, so you might as well take his kidney. If you do, his kidney will never be far from him, that's for sure! They'll be side by side, his two kidneys.

So if you could make an exception, I know I have a lot of donors, but my husband and I would really prefer that you reconsider your decision about him being too old. And just look at him, doctor; he's spent the last forty-five years at my side, just as happy as can be. How could his kidney not enjoy itself inside my body, with my heart beating so close to it? It's only natural.

Down's

I can't believe what you are telling me, doctor. You told me last night, when my son was born, that he was beautiful and perfect and could be loved like any other child. Then you said we probably recognized that he had some features that were familiar to us, like his broad chin and his slanted eyes, but you never said he had Down's syndrome. Why didn't you tell us?

My whole family has a broad chin; you can see it on my face. We have thick necks; it's not that unusual. My wife has Chinese eyes, slanted and pretty, set at an angle. How were we supposed to know you meant our son has a horrible disease? Why couldn't you just spit it out?

You can't imagine how much this hurts us. You are the one who told us, doctor, your son is perfect in his own way. Why did you say that; what was your point? I don't understand, and I can't understand. Your son is perfect and can be loved just like any other child. That's what you said, you never said he has a birth defect, never. You said he was perfect.

Now today, you tell us out of the blue that our son needs heart surgery. That he has a hole in his heart and his blood is backwashing and he isn't getting enough oxygen and you want to take him to another hospital and do heart surgery on him when he's just a little newborn, and then you try to say, like I told you last night; but you didn't tell us anything last night. You never said the first thing about any of this. Why, why didn't you just say it?

All you said was that our baby was perfect and beautiful and could be loved like any other baby. You said we might recognize his chin and his eyes, which we did. Now you want us to suddenly believe that he has Down's syndrome and a hole in his heart and is possibly retarded? How can you do this to us? Yesterday he was perfect and today he suddenly has a birth defect, and we were supposed to know that because he looks like us? Like our families?

Interpreter, do me a favor and please don't be insulted, but could you hand me the napkin that the doctor drew the heart chambers on and the red and blue blood and where he thinks the hole in the heart is? Thank you. Now, excuse me. Harrumph! Harrumph! No, interpreter, don't touch it; let me hand it straight to the doctor. I don't want you to get mucus on your hand.

Here, doctor. This is what I think about your beautiful, perfect baby and your Down's syndrome and your hole in the heart that our son didn't have yesterday. You should have told us. You should have told us right away. Why didn't you just tell us, so we would know? Here, take it! Here's your beautiful, perfect explanation, and here's what I think of it. Take it!

Economist

Although my mother was a widow of limited means, I was attending the university, studying economy, thanks to my relatives in the United States who sent the money for my schooling. I had to take two buses to get to the university, so sometimes I would get home just as it grew dark, around seven o'clock.

One evening, I was walking home, and I had put my foot on the first of our three front-porch steps when I was grabbed from behind. A boy had grabbed me hard around the hips, then another boy was grabbing an arm, and a third boy was grabbing at my shirt, and other boys were surrounding me and slapping and shoving me and pulling on my hair and clothes, and I tried to push back and fight, but I was being held from all sides, held open and vulnerable with no protection, and my books and purse went flying.

I bit my tongue to not scream, not call out, because I knew my mother was inside the house, just behind the door, and if she came out, she would try to help me fight them and then she would be raped or killed. As I struggled silently, I was punched hard in the face and started to fall to the ground. Then isn't life strange? The left-handed rapist.

One of the rapists was left-handed, and he punched me so hard I spun around, and as my face and body swung sharply around to my left, the one light on the street shone on my face, and one of the boys in the back of the group yelled, no! Wait! Let go of her! Leave her alone! It's the economist! The economist! Just like that, the boys let me fall. They turned and walked briskly away, talking amongst themselves, and the last one turned and looked at me sheepishly and said, hey, sorry about that, Miss Economist. That boy, he was from around the block.

As soon as they were gone, I gathered my belongings and knocked on my door and my mother let me in. She was furious with me for not calling out to her for help, but I knew I couldn't let them hurt my mother, and they would have if she had opened the door. We all would have gone inside, and they would have raped and killed us both.

Can you imagine? So that's when we left the country. And I never did get to finish the university. Now I work cleaning hotel rooms to help my mother and to pay back my family for our safe passage. Maybe I will be able to go to school in a few years, but not in the near future. Maybe it's for the best, because when I hear the word economist, I am haunted by seeing that one boy's face, looking back at me, saying, hey, sorry about that, Miss Economist. Can you imagine? Can you imagine having to live like that? People still do.

Eighteen

Sure, I can answer some questions about the pregnancy and my health, doctor. My age? I'm eighteen. Am I married? I should hope so! I'm pregnant. Yes, this is my husband here. Have I been pregnant before? Gosh, no, ha ha! I just got married this year! We haven't had time, have we, honey? No, I haven't had any nausea or vomiting. No dizziness or blurred vision. I haven't been especially thirsty, and I haven't had any bleeding down there. Foul discharge? What do you mean? Oh, a bad smell? No, no, I wash regularly. Oh, you can have an infection even if you have good hygiene? Well, no, in any case no. I don't smell bad.

Do I smoke tobacco? Heavens, no. Drink alcohol? Honey, did you hear that? No, never! Use street drugs! What are street drugs? Like nonprescription drugs, over the counter? Oh! Like illegal drugs, like cocaine! Oh, ha ha ha. Never in my life. Drugs! No, no, no. Never drink, never smoke; we weren't raised that way.

Sexually transmitted diseases? You mean like something I would get from, you know, sexual intercourse? Oh, no. Never anything like that. That would be horrible! Ha ha ha. Can you imagine? Does anyone ever say yes to these questions? If so, they must be miserable. Maybe they're not married ladies, like me. I think it's a little different for them.

You want to test me for AIDS? See if I have what do you call it? See if I'm HIV-positive? Well, I guess it's no harm, but I really don't think I will have it. But I understand; a lot of people here have it. I guess you just want to test everyone, since you can't rely on our word.

No, I'm not mad. I know you have to ask everyone these questions. It's just a little, well, I mean, you must see a lot of strange people, that's all. I mean, pregnant women who have sexually transmitted diseases? Who smoke cigarettes and drink beer? It's not the kind of thing, well, let's just say it's a little unusual to have all these things asked. I know you're saying it's about my health in pregnancy, but, like, no one asked about what foods I eat or how much I sleep, where I work or if I have enough diapers. It just seems a little, well, I don't know.

The interpreter told me, she told me not to take it personally. It's just kind of funny to think of all these people having all these problems, and then some people being mad at me because I got married too young, when I don't have any of these problems you are asking about. So maybe I'm not as young as some people think. You know what I mean? Maybe I'm more mature than a lot of eighteen-year-olds who never had to help their mothers or work in the fields. No, I'm not mad; I'm just saying, maybe things aren't the way you see them, that's all.

Embroidery

I work in machine embroidery, like sports team and company logos on jackets and bags. It is a huge warehouse with Korean owners, and we work very hard. It's cold, and I think that's why I get sick so much. I don't like being cold all day, but that's how it is. The warehouse has such a high ceiling, they say there's no way to heat it. I'm on a big industrial sewing machine.

I get headaches a lot, and the doctor says I have anemia, which is when your blood gets weak. I think my blood is weak from working in embroidery because of the long hours and the fabric dust in my face and the bad lighting and mostly because of the cold.

I am especially thin now because I have lost a lot of weight since moving here. I am single, and I'm staying with my brother and his wife and baby. But they don't have a lot to spare. The deal is my brother takes care of his wife and baby, and feeds and houses me, and I send my whole paycheck home. That way our brothers and sisters can stay in school.

See, we have five younger siblings in Mexico, and my father asked me as the oldest remaining child if I would be willing to sacrifice myself for the good of the others and come stay with my brother here and send money home so that my five younger siblings could stay in school. He didn't make me do it, but I agreed to do it. There was just no way he could keep my siblings in school without my help. That's a bad position for a man to be in.

I want to feel grateful. I mean, with just me alone working, because I'm in the United States, I can support five children on my own little salary. That's because I send every penny to them, and I don't go out to eat or buy myself clothes or anything. If I worked just this hard in Mexico, I wouldn't make but a tenth of what I get here, so I want to feel grateful about that.

But it wouldn't be honest to hide from you that it's hard to leave the warmth and affection of your family, I think especially for me—being a young woman and really missing my mom and dad and my brothers and sisters and all the rest of the relatives and neighbors and my friends from when I got to attend school, when I was a girl myself, not so long ago.

I remember, not so long ago, being plump and rosy-cheeked. I know I didn't have anemia then. I didn't have headaches, and I was never, ever cold. I didn't even know what cold was, I was so innocent. I just lived happily with family, without a thought about the larger world, the world I would have to travel through to come here. Now I have to work eight more years, until I'm thirty, to get my youngest brother through school. And I'll do it. I will. I just wish I could find a job that wasn't embroidery, and maybe I wouldn't be so thin, feel so cold all the time.

English

My husband is Puerto Rican, and he grew up speaking a lot of English. So when he moved to the United States, he fell right in with the English-speakers and ended up not knowing that many Latinos at all. After a while, he started to forget his Spanish. So when we met at church, and he talked to me, we would mix my little English with his awkward Spanish and get to talking that way. And even though I couldn't understand him that much, God put these feelings of love for him in my heart.

When I first realized that I was falling in love, I cried for two days. I mean it. I had gotten out of a very bad marriage and was sure I would never love again. I didn't want to know about or think about men ever again, and then I met this man and started having those feelings. And he was always so respectful; he called me by my formal name and never suggested meeting outside of church. And on the third day of crying my eyes out, I finally said, God, now look. You and I both know I didn't have that much luck last time, and I'd rather not go through this again, unless it's Your will.

So I said, God, if it is Your will that I fall in love again, why have me fall in love with someone who doesn't even like me? I feel like I have to quit going to church now because I can't face seeing him three times a week. It's just too much for my poor, worn heart. But if you mean for me to live with a man again, to have a marital life again, then please, God, send me a sign. Have him show me that he feels the same way, or take this feeling out of my heart.

Well, five minutes later, the phone rings. And I'm still lying on my bed crying. And I answer it, and it's him. It's him, really. I never thought God would work so fast. After all, what is time to God? And he's calling to make a declaration. And I can't understand his English. And he can't find the words in Spanish. So I have to help him. And it goes like this:

I—I want—I will be the man—I want—to know—give chance, you know?

You mean you want to be my man, you want me to get to know you, to give you a chance to show me the man you are, the man you want to be to me?

Yes.

A chance to build a future? With me?

Yes.

It went on like that, and in the end, I think I proposed to myself, but I told him he had to wait for an answer. It isn't good to seem too eager. And now we've been married for nine years.

Epilepsy

You go to a lot of hospitals, since you're an interpreter. Maybe you know if there is another hospital that might be able to help me better. I didn't choose this one; I just had a really bad seizure, and when I came to, I was here. They kept me here for three days this time. I was flown here once last year and once three years ago, and they did these studies on my brain, and they told me what medications to take. Then I went back to Bellingham each time.

The day I got here, the nurse told me she would have a social worker come by and help me fill out paperwork for this program she called emergency medical coupons. The program is set up so if you have an emergency, like my epileptic seizures, then you can get some help to pay the hospital. The nurse told me not to worry about the expense, because the social worker would help me with the paperwork while I was here.

To tell you the truth, I wasn't feeling very well. I still have a headache now, three days later. And I kept forgetting to tell the nurse that no social worker ever came. Then today, when the nurse told me I could go home, I asked her about the social worker. And they called the one who is working today, but she said she didn't have time to help me with the paperwork and I should have asked earlier.

I was kind of surprised, since it helps the hospital to get the money. I will be making payments, but I don't think they will let me have my job back, since I had the seizure there and it makes it dangerous for me to work, and people don't like to see seizures in restaurants. So I will have a hard time paying for all this care until I get better and can get a job again. That's why I liked the idea of the emergency medical coupon.

One question is, where do I go to apply for this emergency medical coupon, since the hospital won't help me? And the other thing is, the social worker said she looked up my record, and I can't just keep coming here and not paying. I need to get in a situation where I can pay my bills before I come back here again, but what can I do when they fly me here unconscious?

So I am thinking that the only way to solve this is to find another hospital where they know how to cure epilepsy. That way I wouldn't have to spend so much on the pills, which I have been taking for years, but they've never cured me. Do you know of another hospital, a better hospital, where they can cure epilepsy? I don't even care if I need to have brain surgery; I am not afraid. Then I could work hard, work anywhere, and keep making payments to the hospital, and I wouldn't need insurance or medical care again. Do you know of such a place?

Example

We are not here because we chose to be here. We were brought here by God, through prayer and thought, until we felt strongly in our hearts, felt sure, that God wanted us here in Washington to continue His work in our Christian community. My wife and I are active members, and we counsel many couples and families on how to reach each other, how to get closer, and how to guide their children lovingly into God's footsteps, onto His healing path.

It is hard for us to be here, since it seems like people center their lives around money and care mostly about acquisitions. We don't see enough couples who find a way to stay home with their children. My wife does. Every morning, my wife takes our ten-year-old to the bus stop and waits until the school bus comes. And every afternoon, she is already standing there waiting for him when the bus comes back. The other day, he said, Mami, promise me you will never stop coming to the bus stop for me, no matter how old I am, because it is such a nice feeling to look out the bus window and see you standing there, waiting to walk me home.

My son told me that some of his friends asked their mothers if they could come to the bus stop like my wife does, but their mothers said, no, I work the night shift, or no, I am too tired, or no, I have to make breakfast for your father at that time. And it seems like a small thing, but it is one more way to tell your child, you are important. You have value. You are a child of God, and you deserve our time and attention. That is the example my wife and I try to set in our community. We spend the time with our child to let him know how important he is, not only to us, but also to God. We encourage him in thinking he is important to God, that what he does matters.

And we never borrow money. That economic pressure of having bills you can't pay, it is enormous. How can you fairly discipline a child, how can you help a child with homework, how can you listen patiently to a child, if you are worried about money, or working a second job, or angry, or scared, or depressed? You can't. You have to be 100 percent behind your family. You have to believe that God has a plan for you and God will make things work for you and your family, and you have to let go of worry and fear. That is the example we try to set, with God's help.

So we love each other, we guide our child by spending time with him, we take care of other children in our community, and we give classes to couples to teach them how to grow closer to each other and to their children. Our classes are very popular because so many people feel alone and long for intimacy. They want to find their way to their loved ones. In our classes, the first step is always, always, getting closer to God. With God's love, all things are possible.

Expense

Our dad had a heart attack, and they put him in the hospital for three days' observation. But he left on the second day, so we still aren't sure how he is, and it was all because of a dumb Spanish-speaking janitor! Our dad never had an education. He and my mom were too poor to go to school. Dad only moved here after most of us had become citizens. As a senior, he was able to get Medicare. Now the government has taken Medicare away from all the permanent residents like our dad who can't pass the citizenship test. Dad can't read, so he'll never pass it.

But at that time, our dad was at the hospital, lying in his bed, waiting for some tests to be run, and we were all working or taking care of our kids, and we had just picked up Mom at the hospital because she was getting too worn out sitting in the chair all the time, and we brought her home to have dinner at home with us, so he was all alone at the hospital for the first time. And then we got a call from him that he had checked out of the hospital.

We were surprised, since they had said they were running a series of tests on him, but we picked him up and figured we would talk to the doctors later. It was about a week later that we found out he had discharged himself against medical advice and he hadn't done all the tests they had asked him to, and we kept bugging him to tell us what happened.

Dad is a quiet, humble man; he doesn't talk much. But we finally got Mom to dig it out of him, and he told her that someone came in the room—he thought it was a doctor, but we found out later it was a janitor—and said to him, you know how much it costs the government to keep you here each day? Each day in the hospital costs the government a thousand dollars.

Well, our dad said, gosh, I don't want to waste anyone's money. I'm not in pain or anything, so I can just go home and be really careful about my heart and take the medicine the doctors gave me. I don't want to be a bother to anyone. He said he had no idea it cost that much or he never would have gone, and we couldn't get him to go back. And now they took his Medicare away from him. So he couldn't go back if he wanted to.

I was so mad! I told our dad, I said, if anyone says something like that to you again, you tell them you have five U.S.-citizen children working their butts off so you and Mom can enjoy some kind of a retirement, and you don't get any money except what we provide. Stupid Spanish-speaking janitor! What business is it of hers to make our dad feel like a beggar? She has no idea what work is, not real work, with her special gloves and her union job and her eight-hour day. She's the one who really needs her heart fixed. And she has insurance.

Eye Doctor

I know this doctor is a world expert on children's eyes, and I know that makes him feel pretty important, but I personally don't think he's that good of a doctor. The other eye doctors, they take the time to chat with my boy, to cajole him to open his eyes, and they let him play with the light first. All the other doctors do. The other ones know how to work with children.

This doctor, he just grabs my son and practically pulls his eyeball out, ignoring his screams and cries for mercy, and it seems like he takes forever. I mean, if he's that much of an expert, shouldn't he be able to look at the eyes more quickly and determine what is wrong with them? Why does he take that long? Does he think my son's eye is just like a marble he can yank out and look at in the palm of his hand? It's my son's eyeball he's grabbing! It's a sensitive thing! It's not just a doctor's toy, a doctor's plaything.

I know I have a mother's heart, and even a regular vaccination hurts me to watch. But this is something different I'm talking about. This isn't just that I am being overprotective or I don't understand about how to get medical care, no. This doctor, he comes into the exam room, and he doesn't greet you. He comes in and just grabs the chart and starts reading it in front of you without even looking at you or your child. He doesn't say anything to you.

Then he starts mumbling things to one of his assistants, and when the interpreter tries to tell me what he's saying, he stops her and says, I'm just instructing my resident; please don't confuse me. I mean, if just hearing his own words in Spanish confuses him, how good can he be? And I understand enough English to know that's what he said: Please don't confuse me.

Then he grabs my son roughly without greeting him, either, and just starts poking and prodding at him without explaining anything, like he found him in a jar in the laboratory. With this look of concentration and cold curiosity on his face. No friendliness at all.

You might not have noticed, but this doctor is extra rough. He grabs my boy's head and holds his hands hard enough to leave red marks. He holds the eyelids so wide open, I am sure it is stretching and hurting. It is way wider than you need to see the eyeball. I think he enjoys hurting people. And he takes forever, like he's trying to say to my little boy: Listen, I'm bigger than you and more important. I'm not going to go faster just because it's hurting you, so why don't you just shut up and quit your crying, you little brat?

Besides, he looks mean. He's always frowning. Expert or not, I don't care what they say. He's not that good of a doctor. A good doctor has to be a good person. And he isn't one.

Fallopian Tubes

My husband has a good job, working for a garden center. He takes care of the plants and does work around the farm. They sell flowers wholesale and grow things to put in your garden. But we can't seem to grow what we want most: a baby of our own. And it's hard to decide whether God doesn't want us to have any, or if we should keep trying.

My sisters all have babies, and my husband's brothers all have babies, so we couldn't understand it. Then the doctor found out my Fallopian tubes are kind of twisted or narrow, so the egg might get lost or trapped along the way. The doctor said it was common. He said he could do surgery to open the tubes up and make them wider. But I had to pay cash up front.

We have insurance through my husband's job, but they won't cover fertility treatment, since they say that it's not medically necessary. So I saved up for it. I worked full-time as a housekeeper for two years, and then I had the cash to pay for the tube-stretching operation. My husband was kind about it and didn't use any of my earnings for the household.

After the Fallopian tube surgery, the doctor put me on Clomid, a hormone treatment that makes you ripen and send down three or four eggs instead of one. But the eggs still can't seem to find their way, even in the expanded tubes, even when they have company and could find their way together. It hasn't seemed to work. The doctor wants to give up on the Clomid treatment.

Now the doctor told me to try in vitro fertilization. They take the eggs out with a long, long needle and put them in a dish. Then they put my husband's sperm in the dish and fertilize the eggs. Then they place the eggs in the womb. It's like getting a ride instead of walking.

The only problem is that it costs something like $10,000 per try, and you need to do three tries, the doctor said. But how could I get $30,000 dollars saved up? How many years at $6.75 an hour would that be, and how old would we be, and by then what would the new price be? The doctor looked like he might cry, and he said that we were just the kind of couple he would like to see have babies, but we still have to come up with the money.

I'm sad I have to try to buy a baby when I wish God would just give me one. My husband says maybe God doesn't want us to have a baby. I can't help wondering, is there something I did that would make me a bad mother? Is that why I can't have a baby? It's so hard to make sense of God's will and decide whether to keep trying or give up. My husband wants to give up, and I want to keep on trying, but what does God want? That's what I don't know. What if God wants me to prove myself by saving up for this, by trying harder to earn a baby?

Family

I am sixty-eight years old now, so it's not that surprising that I would get cancer. But somehow, it's still a big surprise, a big shock, to the family. They were almost more upset than I was, the kids and grandkids and all the rest of them. I mean, I was scared and shook up and all. But like I told the family, the doctor said that having family support can make you live longer with cancer, so with a family like mine, I'll be around for a while, ha ha!

I got married to my husband when I was sixteen. So we started having our kids awfully young. We had seven of them. By the time I was thirty-six, I was already a grandma. Now, I have thirty-seven grandkids and seventeen great-grandkids, if you can believe that. So when we came from eastern Washington for the cancer surgery, we were like a caravan. You know, one of those church caravans with donations and medical supplies that drive to poor countries? Like that, except our cars aren't that good, ha ha!

God has been awfully good to me, because a lot of people love me. So a lot of people drove the four hours to Seattle to wait around together during my surgery, to pray for me and just be there, like we like to do. When they went into the family waiting room, my husband said it was quite a sight! You are supposed to check in at the desk and say who you are and who you are waiting for, and there was a line out the door of people to say they were my family, ha ha! The lady, she got all flustered, like—you, too? And you? And you and you and you? You're all here for her? No, we're not *all* here, my husband says he told her, this is just about a third of us. The rest of us had to work. They'll be here tomorrow.

So she told them, maybe you'd better wait in the cafeteria, because we have limited room here. Then she said most patients bring one person to wait during surgery. She said something about she couldn't believe that I brought so many people. Then my husband told her, it's not my wife's fault she has so much family; I convinced her to marry me young, and one child led to another, ha ha. My husband's a joker. He keeps me going. She laughed, too, the lady.

The family, they ended up staying in the waiting room together. They sang and prayed and joked around a lot and kept good cheer. They gave the lady a couple of tamales and talked with her quite a bit. She ended up really liking us. My husband offered to adopt her, but she said it looked like we already had a big enough family, ha ha! But seriously, I really believe the only reason I am still alive, with this cancer, is because of my family. As far as I'm concerned, there's no such thing as too big when it comes to family. A big family is a big blessing.

47

Family Bed

T he nurses talk a lot about that U.S. disease, sudden infant death syndrome, but I really don't think it could happen to us. Now they say the babies should all sleep on their backs, but I learned from my grandmothers that the babies can strengthen their necks and don't get flat heads if you put them to sleep face down. Also, they don't choke when they spit up in their sleep. And it comforts their tummies to lie face down. My four kids did it, and for my fifth now, all of a sudden the hospital is telling me not to do it, that my baby could die from SIDS.

Mostly, I don't think sleeping position has anything to do with that disease. What I've heard is that it is caused by being scared to death when the poor little babies are left all alone by their white parents. You see, the white parents put the babies all alone in a big huge room called a nursery, and they lock them in and just have some kind of a machine to hear them crying, but I've heard they don't go in when they hear the babies crying. They have these strict schedules they follow, which is why white people always get everywhere on time when they're grown up. They're very punctual. But they are also a cold race, compared to Latinos. We're warmer.

Me, I never agreed with that kind of thing, isolating your babies. Number one, we never had enough room to hide our kids away. Number two, we feel that human beings are social creatures; we need to live in a group and support each other and be warm and loving. We like to cuddle and hug and lie in bed at night talking to our kids, and have family time in bed.

There's this lady in Iceland, a world-famous psychologist; she wrote a book called *The Family Bed*. A bunch of white psychiatrists were getting mad at her at a big international conference, and the delegate from Peru was on the Latin radio here; she said the lady said, "After hearing the concerns and worries of psychiatrists, I have modified my long-held position that all babies should sleep in the family bed as long as they want. Now, I think all kids should sleep in the family bed as long as they want—except children of psychiatrists." You can imagine how mad the psychiatrists were to hear that from a white person! Ha ha. People are white in Iceland.

Anyway, I have lots of kids, and all of them have slept in and around the family bed most of their years, so what's the big deal, really? But I know we live in the United States now, and we have to try to accommodate what people here do, so I did tell my fifteen-year-old daughter who is going into high school this year, "Look, honey, you're not a little kid anymore. You can't be sleeping with your mother your whole life. Why don't you move to the foldout bed in the living room and sleep with your grandma from now on?" So you see, we are trying to fit in.

Farm

Most people I know who work in fish processing in Alaska do it for a reason. They have a sick parent who needs surgery. They have a wife and kids back home and can't seem to get enough to send them a monthly remittance by working in the city. Me, my parents are fine, and I don't have a wife. But I want to save up from a couple trips and buy a farm back home. That's my dream. That's why I go to Alaska, into the puking cold of the ships.

The beauty of working on ships is you get room and board. Especially with housing prices in Seattle, that is a huge deal. A lot of us single guys can't afford our own place, so we stay with a family and work here in town, but you can get into trouble pretty easily, even if you're a short, ugly guy like me, ha ha. You know what I mean; the husband often gets jealous when he sees his wife cooking and cleaning for the young, single guy, who often has more time at the house since he doesn't have to work two jobs to support the children, right? Then the kids start to call you "Uncle." I don't want anybody else's wife; I'm hoping to find one of my own.

That's why I want to save up and get a farm. Let's face it, I'm not the most handsome guy in the world. But a man with a farm, well, that's something substantial. That's something you can offer a woman, to show her you are serious about taking care of her and her children. Take a couple cows for milking, maybe a breeding bull I can rent out to neighbors and use at home. A couple pigs, or even more, I could sell some of them. Chickens by the dozens, and a rooster or two to keep them happy. I am thinking about growing my own corn and beans, of course, but also want to expand out into some of the higher-paying cash crops. No, nothing illegal, ha ha! Nothing like that! I'm thinking about sesame seeds. We use it a lot for candy and cooking, and it is a big item in the United States. But first, I have to get the farm.

Anyway, I have a lot of ideas. When I'm suited up in that big, rubber apron and high-top boots, stuck for sixteen hours a day in the ship's factory, heading and gutting fish until I'm ready to pass out, I daydream about my farm. I think about being able to get on my knee to some nice girl from my village and offer her a future—not just my love, not just my affection, but something substantial. Something that will last her lifetime, and hopefully beyond. I'd like to propose marriage and also tell the woman, I'm planning not only for your own future, for my own future, but the farm will be a future for our children as well. So that's what's running through my head while I'm heading and gutting the fish. The farm. Hmm, I wonder if that's why I cut myself. Hey now, don't interpret that, I could get into trouble! I was just joking, tell them.

Father and Mother

Sorry to be spoon-feeding my wife like this in front of you, but she's just a young thing, and by rights her mother would be at her side now that she gave birth to her first grandchild, and I'm sure her mother would be spoon-feeding her and doing everything to make her comfortable. Her parents are far away, so I have to be father and mother to her now.

This young lady, I can't tell you how happy she's made me when she consented to be my wife. No, don't blush, dear; you're a married lady now, and you have nothing to be embarrassed about. Yes, I was a sick and lonely man before. I cried myself to sleep some nights from sheer loneliness, and me a grown man! I even had diabetes, but since I got married, it went away. It was just the bitterness and loneliness that made my blood sugar turn sour. My blood sugar is normal without insulin now, thanks to her love. And they said nothing could cure diabetes.

Before I got married, every few years, I would go to my parents' village, and they would say, son, you need to get married. You are getting too old. Pretty soon, no one will want you and you'll die alone, no children, no one to care for you. I won't be around forever, my mother would warn me. You need to make your own family now, before it's too late.

I guess I didn't think anyone would have me. I'm not that striking a fellow, just an ordinary person. I don't drink or smoke, thank God. I don't have any vices or weaknesses in the moral sense. But I'm not young and handsome, and I can't dance or anything like that. I don't know how to seek out the ladies. I only met my wife here because she came to visit my niece a lot. After my month in Mexico, I got up the nerve to ask her if she would consent to be my wife.

She agreed, and I went back and got her six months later, and now she has been here a year. But she's been lonely without her family. I know it's hard on her to have no relatives. She's never been through that before. I work two jobs, so she has a long day alone, that's for sure. That's why we tried to get a baby right away, so she wouldn't be so alone.

I'm going home now once she is resting again, and I have all the ingredients to make a huge batch of chicken soup, with three whole chickens in it. I'm going to help her through the forty days of rest after childbirth, make sure everything gets back into place and she is fully recovered. I even bought her the girdle our women like to wear after childbirth. It was a little embarrassing, but when you're father and mother to a wonderful girl like her, you do what you can to make things right. I just bless the day I met her, I'm so happy. That's why I'm spoon-feeding her. So I hope you don't mind seeing a grown man babying his wife like this.

Fifteen

My mother was thirteen when she married and fourteen when she had her first child, so I didn't think it was that bad when I got together with my wife here. I knew she was fourteen, but I didn't think it was that big of a deal. Her mother did, though, and she threatened me and even called the police on me. I didn't realize it was a crime in this country for me to be with my wife until the police told me. I thought the age of consent for girls was the first, you know, menstrual period. Anyway, the police told me that since she loves me and I plan to stay with her, they are not going to prosecute me. So I still consider us married even though we can't get the papers until she turns eighteen.

Now my wife's fifteen, and she's pregnant. Her mother still doesn't like me, and she says twenty-five years old is too old for her daughter, but my father was thirty when he married my mother, and they still get along just fine. I guess it's different times now. I don't want to say anything disrespectful about my wife, and I will not leave her now that I have married her in my heart and she is pregnant, but I have discovered with this baby coming that she is not as mature as I thought. And it is disappointing. It makes me worry about the future. Our future.

For example, this ultrasound they took. The technologist showed us each part of the baby from head to toe. She showed us the blood flowing through our baby's heart. The size of the leg bones. Even some of the parts of our baby's mysterious little brain. And then the technologist took the time to find the baby's profile and get a nice picture of it for us to keep. And the technologist kept working on it until she could get a really nice picture for us.

I was looking at the screen, and why lie? It was hard for me to see because my heart was so full with the coming future, knowing I will soon hold my very own firstborn in my arms. And I wondered how this young woman was feeling, seeing her own beloved child with his tiny little hands waving and moving to and fro over his tiny little precious face, and she said, Look! He's flipping me off! Then she looked at me and laughed, like it was a cartoon and not her own.

I know they didn't have ultrasound when my mother was having her children, and if they had, my father couldn't have afforded it, but I don't believe, I can't believe, that my mother would have had such thoughts at such a time. My mother was a full-grown and very mature and responsible woman by the age of thirteen. Now my wife, at fifteen, is still just an adolescent, and it hurts me. The only solution I can find is to take her home to Mother, back on the ranch, and hope she will mature with God's help under Mother's guidance. But she doesn't want to go.

Finally

The nurse is wondering why I am seventy-three years old and my oldest son is only twenty? Ha ha, well, tell her two reasons. One, I'm a late bloomer. Two, my wife is a cautious soul, and she took seven years to make up her mind. It happened like this.

I had a thriving business back home. Two construction companies, some government contracts. I spent my youth working hard and playing hard. In fact, I had decided there was no point to marriage and I could just stay a lifelong bachelor. I had a lot of friends and family, and my country is filled with beautiful young women, so I never felt the need to settle down. Thus, I spent my twenties and my thirties and half of my forties without a thought toward marriage.

When I was forty-five, we hired a pretty young thing to work in the office. Gosh, but she was pretty! Just the sweetest little thing a man could lay his eyes on, but strict! Strict and stern like a judge or an avenging angel! The first week she worked there, I asked her out for coffee and she was hesitant, but I was the boss, so she went. And when I took her back to the office, I asked if she would like to have dinner sometime, and she said she would be happy to have a business meeting and discuss her job, but nothing more. And she was not teasing. She was serious.

Well, after all those years single, I knew what I was about. I leaned against her office doorway and told her I needed to have a business meeting with her over dinner one evening, and she would of course be on the clock and get overtime, with no strings attached. She came, and I was the perfect gentleman. I never had to force my way anywhere, and I wasn't going to start with this one. So I kept paying her to go out with me each Wednesday evening for seven years. In the end, she knew more about the business than I did, which helped when we were married.

Each Wednesday, she would argue with me. I would tell her, are you sure we aren't dating? And she would say, I'm sure. Number one, the girls at the office warned me about you and your wandering eye. Number two, I would never date an older man. Number three, it's only a Wednesday, and number four, I'm on the clock, and we're talking about the business.

I kept showing her I meant business. I never looked at another girl again, I never flirted, I never rushed her, and each Wednesday when I took her home, I simply kissed her hand and asked if she would see me that Saturday. After seven years, she said yes, and on Saturday, I was on my knees proposing. She was thirty and I was fifty-two. Now we've been married more than twenty years, and she's the same strict taskmaster and beautiful girl I courted and won, and our son is twenty. Luckily, I have Italian blood, so having children late was no problem for me, ha ha.

Five Years

Sorry to keep staring at you, but you look exactly like this interpreter we had five years ago that we lost. We looked everywhere for her; we went to the hospital several times and asked if they could help us find her, but they said, look, we have so many interpreters; there is no way to figure out which one you had. It was at the birth of our son five and a half years ago.

This interpreter, she was so kind to me, more than a family member. I didn't have any family here at all, and neither did my husband, and we were both young. I was so scared and it took so long and it seemed like it was never going to end, and the interpreter helped me so much. At first she was just quiet and encouraging, smiling and just being there.

Then after many hours, when I started telling her, I can't go on, I can't handle it, I can't do this, then she got kind of strict and starting giving me a talking-to, like I think my mother would have done if God would have granted for her to be present with me on that day. Listen, the interpreter told me. You are a mother now, you have been a mother for nine months, and you will be a mother your whole life now; no one can take that away from you. So do you love your baby or not? She asked it like a challenge, like a challenge to me.

I told her, of course, yes, I love my baby. Then she asked me, is there anything you wouldn't do for your baby? No, I told her, there is nothing, nothing I wouldn't do for my baby. No sacrifice is too great. Okay then, she told me. Then do this. Open up and let the baby out. Decide to let go and not be afraid. Be brave and open up and let the baby out.

And this interpreter, she said, do you want to see your baby? I cried, and I said, yes, I want to see my baby. And she said, I can see right through your womb; your baby is anxious to come out and greet you; he has eyes just like yours, and you are going to have a tough time scolding a little boy who looks up at you with your own eyes; it will be hard for your kind mother's heart when you see your own eyes looking back at you. Then the interpreter smiled at me, and we both had tears in our eyes, and I pushed and I pushed and the baby came out.

My husband and I wanted to find her and send her chocolate and roses and thank her for being like another mother to me in my loneliness. It was you? Oh, my God! It's a miracle! I can't wait to tell my husband! You remember? And you're not allowed to take any gifts? It's against the rules? I can't believe it! I've waited five years and a half to find you and give you our thanks, and you can't even take a box of chocolate? Wow. Well. I wish there weren't so many rules to separate people. Well, God will have to repay you, since we are not allowed to.

Follow-Up

T hank you for taking my call. I hope you can help me. You see, I had surgery a while back, a urological problem, you know, with urination. Well, now I have trouble, you know, going to the bathroom and, well, urinating. To tell you the strict truth, I was completely blocked up, and nothing would come out. Do you have a minute? Can you talk?

So I was completely blocked up, and I called the surgeon who did the operation. He didn't call me back. Instead, he had his assistant call me back. She's a social worker at his same hospital, and she speaks some Spanish. She explained to me that she's sorry, but they can't see me for follow-up, since I don't have any insurance. So they can't help me or see me; the surgeon who did the surgery just can't afford it, she told me. She told me to go to an emergency room, because she said they have to treat you, but she said don't come to our emergency room because we already treated you, you see.

I didn't know which hospitals might be a part of the one I'm not supposed to use, so I found a hospital outside of Seattle, and I went to that emergency room. The doctor put a catheter in and drained my bladder, and that was a relief! It had been several days, and it was really painful. Anyway, he put in a catheter, and then he left and his nurse or assistant came in with discharge papers, they called them. She said, listen, at the ER, our only legal obligation is to stabilize you and send you on your way, and now that you have this catheter in place, you are legally stabilized, and we really can't treat you any more. You need to see a specialist who can figure out why you are blocked up, and I recommend the Public Health Department.

So I guess I'm just calling to find out if you have any experts there who can help me figure out what is wrong. Oh, you don't have specialists there, like urologists? Oh. Well, maybe they can just pull the catheter out, and hopefully I'll be able to urinate on my own. If God is willing, I will be able to urinate fine, and then I won't need any more medical care.

I am also hoping I can make payments, because at my restaurant job, they don't offer any insurance. I'll pay for all the care I get; it will just take a long time, since I don't make very much. The other problem is, I am not supposed to leave the catheter in more than three days or it could get infected, they told me at the ER, so I'm hoping I will be able to be seen this week. I'm also hoping I will be better by next Monday, because that's how long the boss said he could hold my job. There are a lot of people looking for work right now, and he can't hold it forever, he told me. So what do you think? Will I be able to see a doctor there? Is there room for me?

Froggie

We had this neighbor in El Salvador we called Froggie because his eyes bulged out. Everyone in my country has nicknames; I don't know why. But the more you like someone, the more you trust them, the more you call them by some special name, a childhood nickname or one you make up. It's like a way of being friendly. And we were very friendly with Froggie. He was our next-door neighbor and my husband's best friend.

We came home one afternoon, and I went into the living room and turned on the television and sat down to watch it, and then I heard a thump thump crash in the next room where my husband was. I went to see what it was, and there were two masked men who had hit him over the head, and he was bleeding and slumped over and they were tying him up, but I couldn't help him because they had our car running in the driveway and they got me outside and they shoved me into the backseat of it and one of the masked men got in next to me and they drove away with me, in our own stolen car.

I was praying, but I didn't dare pray out loud because I didn't want to make them nervous. Also, I could see that the young fellow at my side was trembling, and he looked as scared as I was. Maybe it was his first time. After we drove for maybe an hour, we stopped for gas and that was where there was a confrontation with the police. My husband had gotten free; he had been bound hand and foot and gagged, and he couldn't get his hands free, but he spit the gag out of his mouth and was able to get to our phone and call the police. Since they took our car, my husband could describe it, and that's how the police sighted us at the gas station.

The police started shooting at the car I was still in—shot all the tires—and the fellow supposedly guarding me took off running, and then I saw the driver pull a gun and start shooting back at the police, so I just lay down and hoped for the best and they killed the driver and then a police officer ran up and said, are you okay, ma'am, and I said yes; and after they caught the other kidnapper and put him in another car, they took me to the police station.

My husband met me at the station with a head bandage on, and he said, do you want to know who was behind this? I said yes. And the tears started to roll down his face—and him a grown man—and he said, Froggie, our own next-door neighbor. He arranged it. The boy they caught confessed. Froggie arranged it to get our money. Well. What could I do but sit there and cry with my husband, the tears rolling down my face, thinking that if Froggie could become a criminal, then anyone could, then the whole country has gone bad. And that's when we left.

Frown

Permit me to request your assistance to clarify to the doctor when he joins us that I am an educated person. In fact, I am currently a returning older college student. My employment at a fast-food restaurant is simply to pay for my studies. I would also like you to create an opportunity for me to elaborate on my opinion concerning my medical condition. You do understand what I'm saying? I am not speaking too quickly for you?

Please inform the doctor that I have studied psychology, physiology, anatomy, and other relevant topics already. I know what the doctor is trying to say. I know what they are trying to hint. You do, too. Hypochondria is not an unknown subject to an educated person.

Yes, I have had multiple appointments regarding this matter. I readily admit it. Yes, I have seen my primary doctor, a neurologist, another specialist, and had multiple scans and an MRI done in addition to radiological studies. The fact that they cannot find anything or make a determination to explain my symptoms does not negate the reality of the existence of the said symptoms. I hope I'm not speaking too quickly for you to understand.

I really think it is my facial expression, rather than anything I have said or done, that leads the doctors to believe I am a hypochondriac. I look unhappy. No, you don't have to be polite. I am capable of seeing myself objectively in the mirror, and I am quite aware that I look profoundly unhappy. But it isn't because of my divorce, or being unable to sustain a pregnancy, not that it's anyone's business. I don't know why I even mentioned it. Perhaps as a result of my headache or the painkillers, which can lower one's inhibitions, an unhappy side effect.

It isn't even the fact that I uprooted myself in order to further my education by moving to the United States when my parents sold their home and moved into a small condominium in Rosario. No. It's simply because I was born with a down-turned mouth and a constant frown; it is my physiognomy; these lines represent it very clearly. You may not know about physiognomy, excuse my candor, but the schools here are reputedly rather primitive, so allow me to explain: It's the study of facial features. It's an old and well-known science, I assure you.

In any case, I am sure I have a problem with an obstruction of the cervical nerves running to the right cranium, which gives rise to my symptoms and should be dealt with via exploratory surgery and possible removal of extraneous tissue, I would suppose. About my frown, if I ever become well-to-do again, I shall have plastic surgery and purchase a happy face. Then I will smile all day long. And I will no longer be viewed as a hypochondriac; I am convinced of it.

Frustration

My son has developmental problems. They don't know if the pain pills I had to take for my own condition caused it. God only knows what I have suffered, since I try not to complain all the time, and even if I did, there are no words to describe it. Yet, if there were any way I could go back, I would lie there and scream and cry, biting my pillow and writhing in pain for nine months, if it would give my son a chance for a normal life. I wouldn't care if it put me in a wheelchair; it would be worth it. Imagine if my son didn't have all this frustration!

The doctors say his condition happens to people whose mothers were not on pain pills, too, so I guess we'll never know for sure. His is a very special condition, where part of his brain doesn't communicate correctly with the rest of his brain. He tends to have tics, or call out. He can't learn anywhere near his age level. He can't speak very well in either language.

My son is a sweet, sweet boy. He's like a very young child in so many ways. Some days my own condition is so crippling, I literally cannot get out of bed, and then he will come in and say, don't get up, my Queen, you stay and rest, and I will bring you food; I will bring you anything you need. I'll take care of you, he tells me. How many boys would do that, at his age?

My son cannot say everything he wants to, and he has a tic where he bites his tongue when he's nervous. He gets so frustrated, like he knows what it would mean to be normal, and he wants it. But he can't have it. No matter how hard he tries. The harder he tries, the more frustrated he gets; the more he has tics, the worse he feels. I think he's getting depressed. I see an incredible sadness developing within him as he reaches adolescence now, like he's really seeing how messed up he is, and he longs for normalcy. He just wants to fit in and be accepted.

He told his teacher he was teased by the other kids, but she just told him she hates a gossip. Then he had an incident at school where one of the boys grabbed his backpack and wouldn't give it back. He got to trembling and shaking with rage, and his whole body went into a kind of mild convulsion, and he couldn't find the words in English or in Spanish to get the boy to give him his backpack. A bunch of kids were laughing at him. So my son walked up to the nearest kid, picked him up by the throat with one hand, and held him at arm's length before he put him back down. That child had bruises on his neck. But he was cruelly teasing my son.

The school didn't suspend my boy because they know him, and they know he has a tender heart and he meant no harm. He just gets so frustrated, and he has no way out. Oh, yes, did I mention? No one has taken his backpack since then. And the teacher listens to him more.

God

My father, I don't call him Dad; he beat all of us during our whole childhood. He beat us and kicked us around and yelled and screamed in our faces, and he made us feel horrible, every day of our childhood. We had worries and concerns and fears and tribulations, to use the word from Job in the Bible. I watched my father beat my mom senseless and leave her bleeding on the floor, not allowing any of us to touch her or help her on pain of getting the same treatment. No one can know what all that does to a person. We lived a very isolated life.

My husband has a good idea of what it did to me, because he lives with it. He wants to be close, but when he puts a hand on my shoulder, I jump like a scared dog. I startle at almost everything. And when he wants to take me in his arms, I stiffen up like a board. Nothing is pleasurable for me; I only do what needs to be done to keep my husband; but for myself, there is no joy. Only revulsion and loathing and shame. Lots of shame. And yet I love my husband, I really do. I just can't find a way to express it that is not painful for me. And that hurts him.

My husband, he is more of a man than my father could ever dream of being. He has had great provocation, since I have a lot of rage and guilt inside, but he has never raised a hand to me, as God is my witness. And I have yelled at him, and I have cried, and I have said very mean things to him. But he doesn't fight back. He never retaliates. And it breaks his heart that I am afraid of him; there is nothing he would like more than to have me trust him, to just rest in him and rely on him completely, but I don't know how. It took all the courage I had just to marry him instead of living alone all my life.

About a year ago, I went back to Mexico to visit my family for the first time. My mother had not been well—how could she have been after the life my father made for her? And my brothers who stayed in Mexico, they told us Father has changed. He has found God. He repents of everything he did. He has asked for our forgiveness, too. He doesn't drink, and he doesn't hit Mom anymore. We have all forgiven him, my brothers told me, and now it's your turn.

Well, my father said he was sorry in front of everyone, and he held out his arms to me. I couldn't make myself step forward to save my life. I just looked at him, and he moved forward and hugged me, and I stiffened like a porcupine, every hair on my body raised. I couldn't force myself to lie and say I forgive you. My brothers were mad at me, but what could I do? My father set me up so I will never in my life enjoy the caress of another human being. Now he is an old man, and he wants to hug me. What for? God will have to forgive him, because I will not.

Good Try

Your kids play soccer, too? Your husband coaches? Maybe you can explain something to me. I coach our kids in eastern Washington, where we live, and there's something I've never understood. Whenever the kids on the opposite team do something right, if the parents are white, they will all yell, "Good job!" But whenever the kids mess up, if the parents are white, they will all yell, "Good try!" Why is it a good try when the kids mess up? I just don't get that.

See, being Mexican, we all play soccer, practically from birth. Everyone tries hard and everyone loves it and everyone wants to win, and winning is important. When I coached my son, for the first three years, we never lost a game. The boys took it very seriously. We tried our very hardest. There was no "good try." If it was a good try, it would work. You miss a goal, you lose your mark, you miss a header off a corner kick, there is no "good try." It's a bad job. It's a mistake. An error. The player feels bad. The parents feel bad. Nothing to cheer about.

The fourth year the boys played, they were under twelve years old, all eleven, and they got to the state level of play, and they lost their first game ever. They fought hard, but the other team was better. And let me tell you, when that game was over, every single boy that came off that field had tears pouring down his face, including my son. I had tears in my eyes, too. There was no "good try." There was defeat and sadness, and the boys cared; they cared about winning and they wanted to win, and when they lost, it hurt.

What happened then is the boys tried even harder and they got even better, because no one was standing there among the parents encouraging them to give up, to not try harder, to decide it was a "good try" to lose a game. They came back a few months later, and they beat that same team, the first team that ever beat them. They didn't win by deciding they played a good game and the other team was just better. They only won because they decided they hadn't tried hard enough, and they decided to try harder the next time.

So when you say the parents yell "good try" to encourage the children, I think they probably just don't realize that they are encouraging them to fail, encouraging them to not try their very best, encouraging them to give up and just lose. And soccer is about winning, at least in Mexico. I think for most white people, soccer is just another sport, but for us, soccer is *the* sport. It is the only sport, and we love it and we care a lot about it and we are passionate, and there is "good job," but no room for "good try"—not the way we like to play. We play to win. Soccer builds character, and we don't want to raise our kids to be quitters.

Goodbye

I can't believe our baby is dying. He just arrived yesterday, and now he is leaving. It's so hard to face. It's nice they gave us this room to hold the baby and wait for his heart to stop beating. But it's hard to keep waiting. The poor little mite. I had such hopes for him.

The nurse has come in three times to check for a heartbeat. Didn't they say the baby would die within ten or fifteen minutes? But the baby's heart just keeps on beating. Maybe he'll make it. Do you think he might make it? He's too small, isn't he? He just came out too early, and now he's too small to make it on the outside. Too bad he couldn't have stayed inside longer.

Why do you think he's taking so long? The nurses said he's still alive; his heart is still beating. Why do you think his heart is still beating, since they said it would be very quick? Me? You think he wants to say goodbye to me? I—I don't know. I don't want to take my wife's time with him. She loves him so much. Are you sure it's okay, honey?

Okay, hand him over. Hand him over gently. Don't hurt the little mite. Poor, dear thing. Honey, come sit closer. Come sit right beside me, so we can share him. Look at him. He's so perfect. What a tiny, perfect baby. Look at his face! Why, he looks just like me. My little precious. My son. Blood of my blood. My little boy. Precious babe.

Oh, son, my son! I'm so sorry you have to leave us! I love you so much! I wish to God you could stay. We could have had so much fun together. I would have loved you so much! I would have taken you everywhere. You would never have left my side, son. Oh, my God, this hurts. This hurts so bad! I—I love you, son. I love you so much! I'm so sorry, so sorry, so sorry. Please, I'm sorry. I can't believe you have to go so soon. You just got here. You're so perfect. I just wish you could stay. Oh, my God! This hurts so bad!

Yes, nurse, no, go ahead. You can check his heart again. Can I hold him while you do it? Thank you. Okay, son, she's going to check your heart again. It won't hurt, I promise. Papi won't let them hurt you. I'm right here, son. I love you. I'll take care of you. It'll be okay, son.

He's gone? He's gone. Are you sure? Can you check again? He's gone. Oh, my God. Thank you, nurse. And please, thank the staff for everything, and for this room. Can we sit here for a while longer? Thank you.

Honey, come here. Honey, hold me. Let me hold you. Oh, my God. Honey, did you see that? My boy! He waited! He didn't let his heart stop beating until he came to my arms. The interpreter was right. He wanted to say goodbye to me! He loved me, honey; he loved me, too!

Grandson

I'm fifteen, and my parents have been here for years. So have my brothers and sister, but I was left behind; that's why I still don't speak English. My parents came here to work, and all five of us kids stayed behind with my grandmother. My parents had to emigrate because the economy was so bad. We couldn't afford go to school at all. And we were hungry a lot. So both my parents ended up leaving the country together to work and send us money.

Within a year of them leaving, they were able to get all of us back into school and pay for our uniforms and books and supplies. In our country, if you don't have the right shoes and uniform, they don't let you go to school. That's how so many kids end up not getting their free schooling, and then the government complains that our parents won't send us to school.

After a few years, my parents got their immigration papers and started having some of us join them. They took the oldest first, then the next two, then the next to the youngest. But they left me, the baby, behind. They kept telling me next summer, next summer. Finally, after three years of living with Grandma alone, I got up the courage during a visit to ask my dad, why won't you take me with you? Do you think I won't behave? Do you guys not love me anymore?

My dad looked like he was going to cry. He thought I knew all along that I was Grandma's favorite, because I looked most like my dad, and that I was my dad's favorite, too, and that he was giving me to my grandma as the most precious thing he had to give her in her old age and her loneliness. But I didn't know that until he took me for a walk and told me.

I told him I wanted to live in the United States with my brothers and sister and my parents and go to school there, too, but I would stay with Grandma and take care of her. As it turned out, she died three years later, when I was fourteen, and I came to live with my parents then. My dad cried a whole lot at the funeral, and he thanked me for doing what he could not, for staying with his mom to the end and taking care of her. And I did take care of her.

It was weird at first to come join my siblings when they had all been together without me for so long, but we all adjusted pretty quickly. They help me with my English and talk to me about settling in. One works, two are in college, and one is in high school with me, and we all still live together. We are all pretty close. And a couple of times they have mentioned that it was pretty cool of me to stay back home and take care of Grandma; they treat it like I was doing a big favor for the whole family. So that makes me feel good. But it was a hard time for me, to be left behind like that. Grandma was cool, but why lie? I missed my parents a lot.

Gratitude

Sometimes it's disheartening for me to be around U.S. citizens a lot. No offense to you if you are a citizen, but a lot of citizens just don't seem to feel any gratitude toward their own country. They have this attitude like, I was born here, so I don't have to work for anything, respect anything, or be thankful for anything. Everything is just my birthright, and I don't even have to appreciate it or make good use of it. That's how it seems to me, anyhow.

Take school as an example. So many children, as young as thirteen or fourteen, start skipping school. They start flunking out and just not listening or caring. Meanwhile, I have relatives back home who dream and long for the opportunity to go to school, even for just a few years. They don't even imagine being able to take calculus or Greek history—that would be an unimaginable luxury—they just really want a chance to be able to read and write and do some basic math. But you see, they don't have that chance, because schooling is too far away and too expensive, and we can't afford the uniforms and fees. Yet here are all these kids, same age, sneaking out of the very classes our kids would love to sneak into. It's disheartening and strange and hard to understand, that children here are not grateful for the opportunity.

Take work as another example. I come here and get a job, and I get paid minimum wage, but I don't complain. Minimum wage is more per hour than I would make at home by a long shot. So I work as hard as I can, as if I were making twenty or fifty dollars an hour, even though I'm not, because I'm grateful for the opportunity to work hard and try and save a few dollars to send home to my parents. With two jobs, maybe I will save up and be able to buy a small parcel of land, who knows? But my citizen coworkers are always complaining. They even tell me not to work so hard because I make them look bad! They hate the boss, they hate the job, they hate the pay, and they want everything for nothing, while I just ask a little in return for a lot.

Take citizenship for another example. For me to become a citizen, I have to live here for years and years. Learn English. Pay thousands of dollars. Take a long, difficult test, in English, about the number of senators, the constitution, the whole history of the United States. Then I ask some of the citizens at work, how old do you have to be to become president? How many congressmen does Washington state send to the U.S. Congress? And they just say, who gives a damn, they're all crooks anyway. Why vote when it doesn't make a damn bit of difference?

See, they're born with these rights, and somehow that makes it so these rights don't mean anything to them. I think that's why a lot of people find that immigrants make the best citizens.

62

Greenery

You know that greenery, those pretty, dark-green, shiny leaves they always have in bouquets? That's what we do for a living. We go out into the forest and pick greenery for the wholesale florists. They pay us $2 a bundle. We don't get rich off it, but it's a pretty place to work, and they pay cash every day, and we all get to work together, which is really nice. Almost like being home on the farm, except we don't own anything here. But that's the way it goes. You can't expect to move somewhere new and own anything. That's what I tell my son.

We have a farm back home, but we couldn't afford to run it. The costs got so high and the prices they paid us got so low, there was no way to continue. The family farm is dying, and we didn't want to die with it. We managed to keep our land, though, and I'm grateful for that. I still hope to return there one day. That is my dream, to die at home, if possible.

We are all here now, my son and his family, my daughter, and myself. My husband passed away before we had to leave the farm. I'm glad he didn't have to know about it; he would have worried a lot. But we're getting by. We live on the Peninsula, because we heard it's a lot cheaper to live. But it's hard to find work. It's very beautiful, but it's hard to find work.

While we keep looking, we are picking salal, that bushy plant that grows under the evergreens in the forests on the coast. Like I said, it is used in bouquets. The main problem is that the contractors who pay us don't have a real place to pick it. So we have to go out and find it on our own. We just park somewhere by the forest and make sure it's not a national park so we don't get in trouble, and then we hike up the hillside and start picking and bundling. There's a logging company called Rayonier, but they don't seem to mind.

It is hard work in its own way, not that we're afraid of hard work at all. But you get pretty scratched up and sore, and you have to bend over, and it's hilly and rocky with a lot of undergrowth. Not like working in a planted field on a farm at all. And you have to spend time looking for good spots, and you have to stop to bundle it and make sure each bundle has enough so you can get your $2 per bundle. They won't pay you if your bundle is short.

Sorry I got off topic. I wanted to ask the doctor; my back and knees and hands ache, and the bones in my feet hurt. But I'm not really old enough to quit working. I know I have arthritis, but is there anything stronger I can take so my bones won't ache and I can cut more greenery? Just for another six months or so, until we find something better. Is there medicine? I'm not asking for a miracle cure, just something so I don't feel my pain, so I can work harder.

Grief

I can't believe you're telling me what I had was a grief reaction, doctor, and not a heart attack. You just don't understand how really bad I felt, like dying. Let me explain more fully.

When it happened, I was standing up. I wasn't dizzy. I thought I was just fine. Nothing was going on; no one was there. Then all of a sudden, I felt overwhelmed. I fell in a heap to the ground. I clutched my chest, just like they say happens, you know, during a heart attack.

I was on the ground, and I felt like someone strong was holding me down, with both hands on my chest, right over my heart, just holding me down so I couldn't breathe and I couldn't move. My lungs could not fill up with air. Everything was just shut down and tight, constricted. No blood was moving; I could feel that.

In the middle of this, I felt my arms and hands getting weaker. All over, I was getting weaker. Something burst in my chest—what I mean is, something in here, in my heart, burst or broke loose, something popped open in my heart, like a heart attack. My chest felt like it would just explode and open up, the heart bursting. That's why I'm saying I had a heart attack.

And I lay there, oh, maybe five minutes, feeling the life draining out of me, feeling that I was on the very brink of death, and I took my last bit of strength and forced out a cry, an actual sound. I let out a scream; I don't know how I could do it, how I could force it out, but I did, even though I couldn't breathe and I could feel that my heart was no longer beating; it had stopped. I know I was at the moment of my death, there on the floor.

And when I let out that cry, that one cry, at the sound of that scream, it was like it called the life back into my body, and I didn't finish dying and I was able to stay alive and the strength came back into me. Life flowed back into my veins, and my heart started beating and I still felt that heavy pressure in my chest, but somehow I could breathe in and out again. And although I was still in shock and weak and all, I was able to get up and sit in a chair for a long time. My mom saw I was weak when she came home, and she bought me six bottles of IV liquid, like Pedialyte, and I drank all those, and that revived me. But I still feel bad; I still feel weak, and I know it's my heart. I felt something come loose in there, like something burst asunder.

Just because my big brother—may he rest in peace, the only father I've ever known—died suddenly in an accident doesn't explain why this happened to me. It shouldn't hurt this bad; it's not right, I really felt like I was dying. Something broke loose inside, really. I think my heart really burst or broke and I want it checked, so I don't die from it. It feels like I could.

Grumpy

Y ou know that sweet lady who was married to that grumpy old man? Well, you heard she died, right? You worked with her. I'm sorry you didn't get invited to the funeral. No one knew how to find you. It was beautiful and sad and poignant. It was a real send-off. And I finally saw her husband show some feeling, the poor old man.

They had it at that funeral place up the highway, out of town. They paid I think fifteen thousand for the whole thing—the funeral, the coffin, and the burial plot. But for some reason, there were too many funerals scheduled that day and they got delayed in letting us have our funeral, so when we finally got to the graveside for the interment, it was almost six o'clock.

The staff, they wanted to rush her into the ground, but we argued with them. We told them, it isn't our fault you were running late at the funeral home. We had to wait for you people, and now you should wait for us. We paid a fortune, and we can't just drop her in a hole like she's coming back out later. This is it! She's going down for her final rest, and we have to sing and cheer her on! This is our final chance to wish her Godspeed and send her on her way.

Well, we argued back and forth for the longest time, and the men who worked there were angry. They said they were supposed to leave the place at six and they wouldn't get overtime, and it was getting dark and we had to leave. It was very upsetting, especially to the little girl, who was crying and sobbing, Grandma, Grandma! Then the husband stepped forward.

Nobody puts my old lady in the ground until I tell them to, he told the young men, and his lower lip was trembling as he spoke. He made a fist and held it up, as if to fight the young men off, and he at eighty-two! It was just sad. All of a sudden, we all saw how bereft he was, and how much she truly lit up his life and how he had nothing now. No one had thought he was good enough for her; we just viewed him as a bitter old man. Now we saw his sorrow.

We all wanted to cry and scream out our pain, but instead I started a hymn. And we locked hands around the open grave, blocking the young men from lowering her coffin. And we clapped and sang all the most cheerful evangelical songs, because she was an Evangelist. And we escorted her and accompanied her as far into death as the living can, and sent her on her way. At the very end, we danced and stomped our feet even with tears on our faces, and I swear to you I saw the old man with tears running down his bitter old cheeks like a river as he reached over the coffin for a last goodbye. He must have loved her after all. I hope she knew. God only knows how much he must miss her when she was so full of life and she was all he had.

Hard Work

My wife and I are farmworkers. We have seven children, and all of them work hard. All except this one, the fifth child. I don't know why, but he wanted to study. That's all he has wanted to do. I'm not even sure what he is studying anymore. That's all he's done, though, even now, as an adult. I don't know what he lives on or how he does it, to tell you the truth.

Each of our children, they worked alongside us in the fields. We worked for a Japanese farmer, and he let our children help out around the farm. They each got their high school diploma and then got a job on the farm. Some are mechanics, one drives heavy equipment, but all of them work hard. They know what an honest day's work is like, that's for sure. All except this one. I don't know why, but he never took to hard work. He always had his nose in a book.

This one, he always wanted to study. And since we're a united family, we helped him. Each of us made a pledge to contribute a certain amount each month to his education, and that's what he lived on, plus loans and I don't even know what else, but he never has worked. All these years, he's been studying one thing or another. First he went to Harvard. That's right. Then somewhere in Boston. And now he's going to Europe. Can you imagine? All the way to Europe just to go to school! All he's done his whole life is go to school!

What did he study? Well, that's a good question! I don't really understand much about it. I do know this: When he went to Harvard, he wanted to be a doctor, but after a while, he changed his mind, but I never could make sense of what he wanted to study after that. I don't rightly know. I wasn't sorry he quit studying medicine, though. I actually advised him to quit that and go into computers. I told him, son, doctors don't get rich anymore, not unless they are the one doctor who finds a cure for cancer. But if you don't find it and patent it, you're not going to get rich, and you'll get sued all the time. Why don't you just go into computers—that's where the big bucks come from. You'll be raking in the dough with a computer degree.

I really don't have any idea what my son is up to with all this studying. Seems like he might spend his whole life in school. None of us really get what he is doing, but he sure doesn't seem interested in working hard like the rest of us. He just isn't strong that way. He can't handle it. I don't expect he'll ever be tough enough to really work hard; he's delicate that way. I suspect he'll have to finish all this schooling one of these days and then find a nice, easy job, because he's a bright boy—nobody will deny that—but hard work is probably the one thing he doesn't understand, because you can't learn that from books. God bless him.

Healer

Yes, here's my card. As you see, it says healer and bonesetter. Specializing in diabetes and diseases of the kidneys. I learned it from my grandmother, but the gift itself is from God. All healing comes from God alone; that is the first lesson for healers. We never forget it.

When I was a little girl, people noticed that I never got sick. Others would fall and get bruised or cut themselves, or get colds or even tuberculosis or polio. But I never got anything. Even now, when I'm seventy-nine, I just don't get sick. Never have. People do comment on it.

When I was just a little thing, no bigger than a minute, they found that when I would do sick watch, where you are asked to sit with a sick person for a while, the person would start to feel better in my presence, especially if I laid my hands on them. I was around four then.

My grandmother was already a healer, and she had a huge following and fame. She never charged, of course; no true healer asks for anything because what they have is a gift from God and a responsibility. We're all just human beings struggling along as best we can, and God put us here to help each other. It's a great honor to be a healer.

Grandma got a lot of gifts and money from people in thanks for her services, but she didn't live any better than anyone else; she didn't believe in that. I've lived in the United States for nineteen years. Healing is the only work I've done, and I have my own little apartment that I pay for each month. But I've never asked for payment, I never set a price, and I only take what I know comes from their heart. Sometimes it's just a thanks. Sometimes not even that, if they are nonbelievers and don't trust me, but they don't tend to get well. Not because they don't pay, of course, but because they lack faith. How can God heal you if you deny God's existence?

Now when we found out my granddaughter had diabetes, I tried all the herbs and the remedies I learned, but nothing worked. I don't know if it's from living here that some of the things don't work or if it's my granddaughter's fate for some reason we can't understand. Maybe the herbs are not fresh enough or not picked according to the correct methods. But so many people go through my hands and are healed, even in this country, that it's a mystery.

Sorry to be crying, but it hurts me that I don't have the power to heal my granddaughter. How can she be here, getting evaluated for a kidney transplant, after suffering from diabetes for seven years, when I am a healer and have been able to help so many others? I guess it's kind of like modern doctors, where they're not allowed to help their own relatives. I know we have to resign ourselves to our fate, but I love my granddaughter so much. I really want her to be well.

Heart

Can you repeat that? What is it again? Idiopathic cardiomyopathy? So that's what I have. Okay, thank you, doctor. Just one more thing. Can you explain what that means? I never heard of that disease before. Oh, it's not a disease? What is it, then?

Pathic and pathy both mean disease? So what I have is the disease disease. Well, ha ha. Maybe that's why I've been feeling doubly bad, ha ha. The disease disease. That sounds like someone who stutters. Yes, I've certainly been feeling doubly bad, all right. Myo- means muscle, and cardio means heart? Okay, so I have a disease of the heart muscle disease. I knew that, doctor; that's why I was sent here, remember? So what is it? Idio- means don't know. Well, that makes sense. I mean, we call people who don't know anything idiots. What is it you don't know then? I lost track of things here. What?

Oh. I see. Idiopathic cardiomyopathy means I have a disease of the heart, a heart disease of unknown origin, and you don't know why. No cure known? I see. I guess there couldn't be a cure if you don't know what's wrong. Oh, well, that's the way it goes. Well, thanks anyway.

Honey, don't cry in front of the interpreter. It's not her fault! Heavens. He's just one doctor, and I can see they have thousands in this huge hospital. So what if he doesn't know what's wrong with my heart? He might just be a student for all we know. Is he the expert?

Oh, well, he's not the only expert. That doctor who wheeled me out of surgery, I asked him, do you think if I take my heart medicine, my heart will get better, you know, be cured? And he said probably, he thought so. So see, some of the doctors have more hope and know more.

What? He wasn't a doctor? Oh, ha ha ha. He was just the guy who wheels you around! Ha ha ha. That's a good one. He's the only one who gave me a good medical opinion, and he's just the transport guy? Too bad he's not the doctor; he had a better opinion, but I guess he doesn't speak Latin, so he can't make up those big words, ha ha. That's a good one. The only guy in the hospital with a bit of good news, and he was just making it up. Lord have mercy.

And here we drove four hours to get to Seattle to see this doctor because he is the expert. I tell him I have a heart disease of unknown origin, and he does all these tests and the surgery and tells me in Latin I have a heart disease of unknown origin. I guess I thought I was going to a hospital, not a language school. What is this, Berlitz? Don't cry, honey. Berlitz is a language school. This wasn't a waste of time. We can impress our friends at the orchard with idiopathic cardiomyopathy. Besides remember, now that we're in Seattle anyway, we're going to the zoo.

Heart Transplant

I appreciate your hard work, doctor, and I know you mean well when you say you want to put me on the heart transplant list. But you need to understand, I am very attached to my heart! I love my heart, and trading hearts would be like trading in my old woman here; I just couldn't do it. After everything she's done for me, I wouldn't be a man if I got rid of her. And my heart, well, it has kept on faithfully beating all the days of my life. It would be horrible to just take it out and throw it away like a piece of garbage!

Oh, I understand, my heart is weak. My heart is old. My heart isn't as strong as it used to be, and it isn't working all that well. But it's my heart, doctor! If I love my wife, this old lady, so much after most of my adult life with her, how much must I love my own heart that has been with me from the very beginning? There's a lot of love in this heart, not just blood. I know you might not believe that, and you've looked at hearts and cut them open, but that is what we believe. Our hearts, that's what we feel with; that's where we keep our love.

We read in this magazine about this man who had a heart transplant and he was a vegetarian from India, and when he woke up, he was so hungry for a cheeseburger and fries. And he never even wanted to eat meat before the surgery. And then he found out the heart he had, it was from a nineteen-year-old boy who had a motorcycle crash right after he ate his favorite meal at McDonald's: a cheeseburger and fries! This was in the real news. They can't explain it.

So I appreciate your wanting to help me, and I appreciate your saying that I really think with my brain and that's where our feelings come from, and I know you've seen other heart transplant patients and they are still the same person, but I don't know, maybe it's different for Latinos. Maybe we keep more in our heart— we are called a warmhearted people—maybe we use too much blood, and it wears our hearts down young. I know a lot of Latinos have heart disease.

Anyway, I really, really respect you, and I know you have a lot of education and experience, but with all due respect and without wanting to offend anyone or seem ungrateful, I just thank you very much and all, but I don't want to have anyone else's heart. I'll go when my time is up. I understand what you said about longevity, doctor; I'm not asking for a miracle. But I'm telling you sincerely that to give up my old heart that has been beating for me since the day I was born, well, that would be like getting rid of my dear old wife here, after everything she's done for me, and that just isn't right. I can't find it in my heart to do it, ha ha. You know what I mean, doctor; did that one make a joke in English, too? Did you get it?

High Protein

Yes, my husband and I are both here for the ultrasound to see what's wrong with the baby, because I have extra-high protein in my blood. They had us meet with the genetic counselor to talk about what could be wrong with the baby and what are the risk factors, she called them. She asked us all kinds of weird things, like: Was I ever a farmworker, did I clean up cat poop, and was I possibly my husband's sister? They must meet a lot of strange people in their line of work to think those questions are not perplexing and offensive! Excuse me, but I think I'd know if I married my brother, or even my halfbrother. My dad wasn't that kind of man, and neither was my mother, may she rest in peace. And my mother-in-law would break me in two if I ever asked her that kind of question! God forbid!

Thank you for being with me in this ultrasound. I know they can't tell us everything they see; they already told us it's against the rules, and the radiologist has to read it in private and then he tells my doctor later. But it's awfully hard to wait for two weeks until my next prenatal checkup, so I was hoping if maybe you chatted with the technologist, since you know everybody, why then, maybe she'd give you a hint, and you could give us a hint. We'll love our baby no matter what, but it would help prepare us. We need time to become resigned to our fate.

You know the genetic counselor, the young one? Well, I don't know what kind of counseling degree she has, but I'm telling you, I haven't met a more ruthless woman. She told us our baby might have Down syndrome or a couple other things like an incomplete spine or water on the brain or something, and then she told us we can kill it if we want to. First she asks if I'm committing incest, then she suggests I commit murder! This is a woman I've just met! Think how she'll treat someone like a daughter-in-law who she actually wants to hurt and put in her place! I feel sorry for whoever marries her son! I honestly do! What a life she will lead!

Could you just ask them to tell us, just anything at all, what they are seeing? Chat with them? Is the head extra large and flat? Can you see if the spine is complete? Can she turn the screen so I can see? What? Two heads? What? Oh, my God. Oh, my God! Thank you, Jesus! Thank you Blessed, Blessed Mother of God! Twins! And they're okay? Honey, did you hear that? We're having twins! That's why the protein was high in my blood! There's nothing wrong with them! It's twins! Thank you God and Mary and Jesus and all the Saints. Thank you, thank you, thank you. Thank you, Blessed Mother. Twins! Anyone have a Kleenex? Two perfectly healthy, perfectly matched twins! And she thought we were brother and sister! Ha!

Home

I know a lot of couples bring their children to the United States when they come here to work. But that just isn't something my husband and I ever considered. We don't think it's the best place for them. As parents, it isn't our job to just do what feels good to us, like take them with us so we don't have to miss them. Our job is to do what's best for the kids, and that means leaving them home. Leaving them home and sending them money.

Here is what it's like for our boy and girl. They get up in the morning, and they are greeted by the smell of their grandma's coffee and eggs in the kitchen, with a pot of beans already on the stove. Grandpa is sitting at the table, prepared to go out and do some chores around the farm. Several of their uncles, their aunties, and cousins also join them at the table. Then they get ready for school and take the bus into the village with their cousins.

The children have school until noon, then take the bus home and do chores and homework. Then they play, without worrying about language or traffic or kidnappings or money. They just go outside and have their childhood. They have fruit trees, and places to play and climb, and shady spots they can hide in, and they have bedrooms they share with their cousins. They have lots of people to hang around with. And they are surrounded by loved ones, which is the most important thing.

If they came here, what would they have? My husband and I would have to switch schedules so one of us would be home all the time, to avoid day care. We would earn less money. They would have to go to a school where they can't speak the language. They wouldn't get the wholesome farm food they eat there. They wouldn't be able to roam freely. Even to go to the corner park, kids have to go with their parents because there are all kinds of big-city dangers that our kids have never even heard about.

Even if we decided it was a good idea, like if our children were older and we wanted them to come here for high school, we would have to pay U.S. prices for their clothes and food and medical care. We wouldn't have anything left. We would never get ahead. And soon enough, the kids would speak English and ask for expensive clothes or Game Boy, and then all of sudden, we would be deported and how would the children handle being back in Mexico? They would never feel at home. The whole point of leaving them home is so they have a home, a sense of belonging, a place they can say they are from. God willing, we'll join them there in two years, and then we'll all be home together, with a nest egg and no harm done.

Hunger

I've been ill for a long time, and the doctors say they can't tell me how my disease started and why I am disabled, but I can't help wondering if it could be caused by childhood suffering and starvation. Hunger. Hunger.

We were a very large family, twelve children, and we never had enough to eat. The conditions of our life didn't allow it. So instead of five or six tortillas with our main meal, we would have one tortilla, or sometimes less than a whole one. Instead of beans with onions and peppers for flavor, fried in oil and topped with a little grated cheese, we would have a little half-cup measure of beans boiled in water with just salt. Forget peppers, onions, cheese, even cooking oil or lard. Those were luxuries to our family, unattainable luxuries.

Meat was something we didn't really know. Sometimes, when we were very lucky, a pious neighbor would give us a piece of something, maybe once a month, and my mother would cook it up in a big huge pot. But then my father and the oldest boys would eat the meat, and we little ones and the girls would get broth with beans. The men needed it more, since they did the hard work in the fields. We hardly ever saw rice because it was just too expensive for us.

When I talk about hunger, I don't mean the hunger you think of where you say, uh-oh, I accidentally skipped lunch and my stomach is rumbling. I don't mean a plump lady trying to skip dinner to lose a couple pounds. No, I mean hunger. Real hunger. Where your little belly is empty and it starts to eat itself, and it is a burning hole and you can't think about anything else. You can't play and you can hardly help your parents work, and you can't sleep and you can't even think about anything else but your hunger. If you fall asleep, you dream about food.

As little children, we experienced true hunger almost every day. We ate the simplest of fare, but never enough. We never had a chance to say, no thank you, I'm full. We never had a chance to make that little movement where you push your plate away and the hostess knows not to keep serving you. We were never, ever truly full. Our little stomachs hurt every day.

Even now, when I'm too ill to work, I insist that we have plenty of food around. We might not own a lot, but my children know what it feels like to be full. They can pick and choose what they like, and nothing is measured out or limited to them. The first time my son said, I don't like this food, I burst out crying. My wife thought I was upset at his bad manners, but I was just so glad my son had the luxury of not liking food. That's when it hit me, like a gift from God, that my children have never known hunger. Imagine the luxury of saying no to food!

Hurting Myself

The doctors keep asking if I want to hurt myself. Every day, we have a meeting and they ask me, do you have thoughts of hurting yourself? Do you feel like hurting yourself? Would you like to hurt yourself today? Could you try to explain to them for me; it isn't like that. It's a horrible, overwhelming fear that makes me so terrified that I want to make it stop. See, I'm not trying to hurt myself; I'm trying to make myself feel better, to end my pain. That's the only reason I wanted to kill myself. Not to punish myself or hurt myself, just to end the pain.

Because of what happened to me in my country, what I saw during the war, I have a lot of things inside of me that I thought were gone, but they're not. They just keep coming up. And the more I try not to think about them, the more they invade my mind and keep intruding into my thoughts. And I hate myself for losing control, for not being stronger, for not being able to force the past back into the past. Then suicide seems like an act of mercy, a way to end the suffering.

I get scared to go outside, and then I make myself go outside, to force myself to handle it, because I am sick of my own weakness. Then I find myself shaking like a leaf, losing control. I am terrified, and I break out into a cold sweat. I feel like everyone is looking at me, laughing at me. Like everyone knows my suffering and doesn't care. Just like then, I start to look around, and it seems like the people I see think I deserve my suffering, and no one lifts a hand to stop it.

When this thing comes upon me, it is like waves and waves of pain that seem unending and unendurable. I double over. I feel nauseous. Sometimes I vomit from pure fear. I get diarrhea and horrible cramping. My hands break out into a cold sweat, and my heart beats so hard I think it will burst into a thousand pieces and I will just bleed to death, inside. My heart seems to be beating itself into an explosion of pain and blood.

Then I think about that happening, my heart bursting and breaking from the pain, and I think maybe it wouldn't be such a bad idea. And I think about pills or accidentally on purpose walking off a curb in front of a bus, but then I feel sorry for the bus driver—why add to anyone's suffering? There is enough suffering in the world without adding to it. So I think about how to end my pain without hurting anyone, without hurting myself.

That's why I tried to kill myself. Not to hurt myself, you understand? To protect myself, to protect myself from ongoing pain and suffering, to put an end to it, to protect myself. Please explain that to the doctors, if you can. I just don't see a better way to end my suffering. I don't see it. They can call it post-traumatic whatever-they-want; that doesn't make it go away.

Hysterectomy

I don't understand why they're asking me to consent to a hysterectomy now. When they did the cancer removal, the tumor removal, the surgeon said no hysterectomy. He told me, you're barely thirty. There's no reason to take out the whole plumbing down below. You're going to get other health problems in the future if you're missing that part; you know what I mean. Like leaking or growing a mustache, or something. I don't know what all. He didn't really explain it.

So I went for the radiation and the chemotherapy, and I had to wear this appliance called an expander to hold my private parts open because they say the radiation can burn it up and it can get stuck shut and then you have a real problem down below. So I wore it, but I can tell you it was not comfortable. It is bigger than a man's organ, and it's not soft and fleshy. It's stiff and feels horrible, like that steel duckbill they put in you for your Pap smear, except you have to keep this expander thing in all night. They were saying wear it sometimes in the day, and I am thinking, waddle around all day? Haven't I been through enough with cervical cancer already?

Now out of the blue, they say another surgery, so I figure they'll look around for any tiny specks of remaining cancer and pull them out—like removing a mole kind of size, I was thinking. And now they say no, they mean full hysterectomy. A full hysterectomy! Womb and ovaries!

I'm a young woman; at least I was one before I found out about the cancer. We only have the one daughter, you know? A girl, God bless her, but my husband, well, you know how men are. He wants a son, too. So I told the doctor, this isn't going to work out for me, since our plan was to go through the chemo and radiation and wait a year to be safe and then get pregnant again. And now they say, well, you can never do that again, because all your eggs are sterile and your ovaries will never work again and the lining of your womb is burnt out and nothing will work anymore, so we're just going to take it all out, and then we can look in the pathology lab and see if any cancer is in it, but we can't put it back in afterwards.

Well, I guess if they already wrecked and burned everything, there's no point in keeping it inside of me, but it would have been nice to know all that ahead of time. The doctor says she thinks she told me before my first surgery, but she thinks I was confused and forgot. Excuse me for being so frank, but I don't think I'd forget something like not being able to give my husband a son, no matter how confused they think I was. I'm not some old, forgetful grandma. I was a young woman then, in the middle of having my family, before all this.

Ice

Everyone recommends that same drug and alcohol counselor, but I don't like him, and I can't like him. He is as cold as ice. He just stares at me with a frowning, serious look, like a funeral director. He just bores holes into my eyes and glares into me. He acts like he's the only one who really knows how to live, and what to do. He is trying to get my husband not to drink, but he doesn't understand how to go about it. He has a cold and distant way about him.

I know my husband should drink less. I know he should probably not drink at all, because he does drink too much. But he never beats me. He isn't vulgar. As far as I know, he isn't going out with other women. No. He just drinks to relax. I know he drinks every day, but it's not like he's a really bad drunk like so many people you see. He's not like them.

But this counselor, he treats everyone the same. He acts like alcohol is the root of all evil, and no one should ever have anything to drink, no matter what. He says anyone who drinks too much is an alcoholic. But my husband is a good man. He works hard. He doesn't miss work to drink like other men do. He doesn't go to work drunk, either. He only drinks after work and then on weekends. Okay, on weekends he might be drinking during the day, also, but so what? It's his only day off, since he works two shifts and only has Sundays off regularly. What's so bad about trying to relax? He does drink a lot, but he isn't hurting anybody.

This counselor, he met with both of us, and he told my husband, you are an alcoholic. You are a drunk like any other drunk. You need to get inpatient treatment for one month, then intensive individual therapy, then ongoing group therapy, and all this while, for this two-year period, you should be going to AA meetings—first every night, then three times a week, and after a year, you can cut down to twice a week if you haven't had any relapses, he said. I don't remember the exact schedule, but it was something like that.

Now, the counselor knows I'm home pregnant and ill. He knows I can't work. So I asked him, Sir, who is supposed to support me while my husband lives in the hospital, and how is he going to keep both his jobs if he is going to meetings all the time? We have to eat. We have to keep a roof over our heads. And now we'll have this baby to support.

So the counselor, he said, look. Like it or not, your husband is going to die if he doesn't get treatment. It's this or nothing. He is not going to be around to raise the child you're carrying. He is a late-stage alcoholic, and they have two choices: Get treatment or die.

Is that any way to talk to a pregnant lady? The man is as cold as ice, I'm telling you.

Identity

S omeone stole my wife's identity. I told the government, but they're giving me the runaround. No one seems to care but us that my wife seems to have an evil twin living and working in Idaho, using my wife's name and Social Security number.

The way we found out is, we filed our taxes, and then the IRS wrote us and said you owe all this money. We went to a hearing, and the IRS officer told us, look, you have all this income in Washington and all this income from Idaho, and you earned a lot more than you reported, so you have to pay more taxes. And you can get penalties and late fees, since you failed to report this income from Idaho.

I told the guy, we have never been to Idaho. How can my wife be working there? Plus, she works full-time here, in Seattle. Do you think she flies down there at night to work? Don't you understand it is a question of stolen identity? Isn't that obvious? If my wife here were the fake one, I wouldn't be married to her. So why don't you just arrest the fake one? Simple.

Well, now, the IRS guy told me, it doesn't work like that. I suggest you contact Immigration. If you can prove to me that there are two different people, then I can let you off on your taxes. So I called Immigration. I gave them the fake one's work address, and they said, yes, it's a problem, but we don't have the resources to hunt down individuals like that. Every illegal alien in the country has a fake identification. It's not that easy to just round them all up.

Immigration told me to call Social Security, and Social Security told me to call the IRS. So this is how it's been going. If you can believe this, the best idea that Social Security had is for me to send this Mexican restaurant a copy of my wife's Permanent Residence card so they will know that the lady they have working there is the fake. Like they don't know. Like they wouldn't love to have a copy of my wife's real Immigration card with her Permanent Residence number and her signature on it. Everyone's basically telling me I have to fix it myself, but I don't carry a sheriff's badge. What am I supposed to do about it? I'm no vigilante.

The IRS appeals guy finally said if I can prove that my wife was never in Idaho, he'll take away our back taxes. But he said it's up to me to prove it; he doesn't have a legal obligation to look into it himself. So now we have to get her employer to sign a letter with all the dates she worked and get letters from church and other people who have seen her around in Washington state. I told the guy, I'll check our broom closet, but as far as I know, my wife doesn't fly a broom to Idaho to work the night shift at Las Margaritas.

Jalisco

People always talk about how they know we all came here for a better life, but they don't understand. It's not that simple. We are just as poor here, but in a different way. It's not all so much better. But because of the cash, the dollar, the whole money thing, we get caught up in it, and it's hard to stop and say, enough is enough. Let's go home. By the time we've saved money, we've changed. We can't leave until they make us leave, until they deport us.

I'm from Jalisco, and we were poor, Mexican poor. But we never went hungry. We always had enough to eat. We had a strong, united family. We had a lot of fun together. We ate well. We had parties. We danced. We had big meals, like barbecues and picnics and celebrations. People wore their best clothes, made by a local tailor, and the ladies felt good about their one good dress. We wore the same dress to parties until it was worn to threads.

We got hungry—well, there was always beans and rice, plenty of corn. We had company—well, you don't go to the store; you just catch a chicken and make a meal that way. Even people who didn't have a good crop, or didn't keep animals, they would just go up into the hills and come back down with big bags of nopal, a kind of cactus. It can be eaten in a bunch of ways, and it's free—all over the hills. Here, you buy a tiny little glass jar of nopal, and it's $4.59 at the Mexican store. It just tastes like broccoli, has no flavor left. You can't do anything with it; you just eat it for sentimental reasons. It doesn't have any flavor.

Here in Seattle, we're United States poor, you know what I mean? We don't have our family around. We don't have our traditional foods. The beans, the rice, they taste different. You can't get good tortillas, and you can't always get good masa, the fresh-ground corn, to make them from scratch, and you don't have time anyway. Time, we are time poor now.

I work full-time, out of the home, so I am gone eleven hours, five days a week. My husband works sixty or seventy hours a week in two different restaurants. My kids are in school, then they come home and do homework, and my daughter has to start the evening meal, since I will be so late. But then she complains about it; she says, Mami, I don't have any time!

Finally, I told her, listen, honey, you want time, you go back to Jalisco. You'll have plenty of time there. No, I like it here, I just want more time, she told me. I told her, well, you're never going to get it here; time is just what nobody has in this country. They trade it all for money and then buy things they don't really need. You want time, I told my daughter, you go to Jalisco. But she won't, you see, not until they catch us and deport us.

Jealousy

I fell because of him. But he blames me, and so does my brother. My brother says to me, you can't be jealous. You know how men are, even me. You have to be understanding. You have to look the other way. A man comes here to work like a dog—sometimes two jobs—so when we go out, for heaven's sake, we want to joke around with our buddies, forget ourselves for a moment, have a beer or two, and just relax. You need to look the other way, he told me.

I'll admit I'm jealous, but not without reason. We broke up for a while because we argued a lot, and during that time, he went out with a friend of mine—or I thought she was a friend—and my best friend went along, too. Just to go dancing, supposedly, but they ended up drinking a lot, and I never drink. And they stayed over, all three of them, in my boyfriend's room after the party. And my best friend, she says she saw the two of them having actual intercourse shamelessly right before her eyes. Like dogs.

My best friend told me about it just last month, and he of course denied it. Then she came over and accused him to his face, and he still denied it. But I knew it was true; I could tell. I made him move out, and then my brother kept bugging me to give him another chance. My boyfriend's from our same village and we've known him since childhood, and my brother said he feels better knowing I'm with someone we already know. He said it was a long time ago that he cheated on me, when we were in a fight and not together, so I should just forget about it. Now that I'm pregnant, he said, I need to handle the situation like an adult. He said I'm immature.

Well, I took my boyfriend back and then we went out for the first time last night, and the first thing he does when we walk into the party is grab his friend from work's arm and start elbowing him and pointing to this dressed-up woman and making all kinds of comments and giggles and whispers, and me six months pregnant and fat as a whale and just having forgiven him, and I blew up! We argued, and he got so mad, he left the party. He just literally left me with no car, no money, no phone, and no way to get home, after yelling at me in front of everyone. I was so humiliated, I just walked out of the party.

Tears were streaming down my face and I was just stumbling along, and before I got a block away, I fell and started cramping. I walked until I found a pay phone and was able to dial 9-1-1 without a coin, thank God, and that's how I got here. Now they're trying to stop the baby from coming, and my boyfriend—well, you saw it—he only came in to tell me it was my fault I fell, not to apologize or even ask if I'm going to lose the baby. What's going to happen to me now?

Joking Around

When I was growing up in Mexico, a father was a man to be feared and respected. I raised my kids the same way, teaching with the belt what they wouldn't learn with words. Then I came here alone to work the fields and send money to my wife and five kids. I would travel home once, maybe twice a year. I paid room and board to another Mexican family and ate my rice and beans and sometimes chicken with them, you know, just like a family member. And I started to see how families here treat their kids.

One thing I noticed is it seemed like there was less respect, and I definitely didn't like that at all! But I also saw something curious. More affection. The fathers and the kids acted like they were buddies and joked around together in a friendly way. I saw a lot of kids, good kids, who went to school and worked alongside their fathers, but still joked around a lot with them, like friends. And the fathers let them. They didn't scold them about it.

Once I hurt my back after that ladder gave way when I was pruning trees, my wife sent me my oldest son to work for me while I recovered. He was seventeen. When he first arrived, it was yes, sir, and no, sir, to me. He didn't open his mouth unless I asked him a direct question. But then he saw how the kids here are pretty relaxed with their fathers, and he kind of loosened up, and so did I. And we started joking around a lot, like the other families here.

For example, I was telling him, son, you'd better quit wasting your phone card calling your girlfriend back home; a young, plump thing like that isn't going to wait around forever; you know there are guys lining up to spend time with the girls whose beaus are out of the country working. They'll be happy to spend the money you send her. And then he says, well, Dad, you'd better watch out yourself, because Mom looks as good as she ever did, and you've been away even longer, so you'd better think about getting down for a visit soon. They'll be lining up outside our house, too.

Back in Mexico, for a joke like that, my son would have received a whipping he never would have forgotten! Joking about his mother, joking about my honor. But since we're sort of like buddies now, I knew all he meant was he really, really likes his girlfriend, and he can't stand to think about her being unfaithful. And instead of getting mad, we both just laughed together for a long, long time. And I quit teasing him about his girlfriend and started calling her my daughter-in-law. Joking is fine in its place, but you have to know when to quit joking, too.

But you know what? My son is lucky we weren't in Mexico. Damned lucky.

Joy

I can't believe this is me, in childbirth—me, who just over a year ago thought I would never marry. I was happy in my—here comes another one. Help me! Help me to breathe!

Okay. I was happy in my life; I had a nice job in an office, and girlfriends to visit with, and I lived with my parents in their home, and I didn't really look for more than—here comes another one. Okay, I can handle this. I—

Okay. Whew! Oops! Here comes another—oh, God. Oh, Mother Mary, I pray to Thee for strength. Oh, dear. Here, here we go. Whoo. Whoo. Whoo. Hee. Hee. Hee. Honey, take my hand.

This man here, he talked me into marrying him. I hadn't known him long. But he was looking for someone like me, someone decent, and I thought I was kind of old, being in my—here it comes again. So many! So close together! Is that normal? That won't hurt the baby?

I'm older now and didn't really have a thought toward marriage. I never expected to have my own children. And here I am. My blood pressure is up, but I know it's just from the pain. No, I can handle it. I don't want medication. I'm fine. Okay! Here comes another one.

Whee. Whee. Whee. Okay, okay, I can handle this. Look. Can they check me again? I just want to know if I'm getting any closer. I feel like I am. Thanks.

Really? Praise our Heavenly Father. You think I can push? It won't hurt the baby? I don't want to hurt the baby. Oh, dear. I can't believe it. Here comes another one. Hold my hand, honey. Here comes another one. Here it comes. Okay, I'm bearing down now;, I'm going to bear down. Help me hold my legs back. I can't hold them and breathe at the same time.

Oh, Lord. Mother Mary, help and guide me. All the Saints of heaven, come to my aid now in my time of need, help your humble—here comes another one.

Oh, oh, oh, oh! I feel something here, in my chest! Oh, here, here, in here! No, no, it's not hurting. No, it's here, here, I'm feeling it here. That's why I'm crying. Oh, my God, dear God! It's—it's joy! Praise and thank everything and everyone! I'm just so grateful! I'm going to have a baby! Thank God! I just keep hitting my chest because there's so much joy! Oops! Here comes another one!

Oops! I scared the midwife! Tell her, I'm not having chest pains, I'm not having a heart attack or anything, I'm just feeling so much joy! That's why I am hitting my chest and—here comes another one. Okay, hold on, everybody. Get ready for more. What joy!

Junior

I had a lot of dreams for Junior. A lot of dreams. When you are a man and you find out your wife is having a little boy, it's something. When you have a girl, it's like you now have someone like your wife, a precious person to love and protect. But when you're a man and you have a son, it's like there's going to be someone just like you in the world, only better. Someone beyond yourself and greater than yourself. It's a big thing, a powerful thing.

When we found out Junior had cancer, it was, no. No. No. Uh-uh. No. No. No, that's wrong. That can't be. There has to be another reason; maybe he has some other thing, something you can take vitamins to fix. No. No, it can't be. No, not cancer. Not Junior. Not when he's too little to even go to school. Too little for kindergarten. No. It's a mistake.

This little fellow, he's my replacement. He has my name. He is my better self. He's here to carry on. To be more than I ever was. To do everything. Go to school, all the way through. Any kind of job he could imagine; he's smart. He can learn it. Any kind of job in the world, he can do it. Anything he wants to be, anything he wants to do, I can help him. He's going to have every chance in the world. All the chances a person needs to really get somewhere, to be something. To live all the life they have. To get somewhere good.

I was planning, I was dreaming, of helping him with all kinds of things. Going to parks. Playing soccer. Fishing. Even cooking and working in the yard. And I would coach his soccer team. And I would be at every school concert. And if he wanted to play the piano, I would find a way to buy him at least a keyboard. And if he needed help, I would always be there to help him, help him get where he needs to go. And this would go on for years and years and years.

Now this is what I do. I sit by his hospital bed. I stroke his head when it doesn't hurt him too much to be touched. I sing to him. I stay with him. When they take him for his radiation, I pick him up all wrapped in his favorite blanket. I hold him in my arms and I hold him still, and I try to comfort him while he cries and tells me, don't let them, Papi. Don't let them do it again, Papi, please, Papi, I don't want to go to sleep. Don't let them, Papi, please, Papi.

Then they put him to sleep again, and I lay him gently down on the radiation table. And when he wakes up, they put him into my wife's arms, and she holds him while he wakes up, and I just sit there. I just sit there beside him and think, this is not all the fathering I wanted to do. There is so much more in me. So much more to give. I have years and years and years of fathering inside of me. And it hurts. What good is a man who can't protect his own son?

Keeping House

I love keeping house. I hear a lot of ladies here complain about it, but to me, it is a great pleasure. Of course, everyone wants to live in a nice, clean home, but I also enjoy the process, the motions and steps of keeping house. It's fun, like playing house when you're a little girl and dreaming of a home of your own, a nice home you can keep clean.

I sweep the kitchen every day, since the children are small and I wouldn't want one of them putting something into his mouth off the floor. I also vacuum just the center of the living room rug every day, the part where the children like to play. I load the dishwasher and run it every night, so there are no dishes just sitting around smelling up the house. That's daily.

Then I have a weekly routine. Saturday morning, I get up extra early and do all the quiet jobs while the family sleeps. I wipe down the kitchen cupboards and countertops and sweep and mop the floor. I make sure the fridge and stove surfaces are clean and shiny. I clean the bathroom sink, tub, and toilet. And I pick up the whole house, putting each thing in its special place. I have everything organized so it fits, even though we own so many things now.

Once the family wakes up, I feed them breakfast. Then I can do the noisy things, like vacuuming, laundry, opening and closing drawers and closets—that kind of thing. Then each week, I choose an extra chore, like cleaning the oven, defrosting the little freezer, wiping down a wall where the children have gotten fingerprints, or dusting the pictures on the walls. If I get up early enough, all this is done by lunchtime, and I have the rest of the weekend for play.

On Sundays, the house is already nice. I light candles. I cook Sunday's dinner on Saturday night, since I don't believe in doing work on Sunday. I do believe it's okay to heat food up on Sunday, just not to cook it. So I rest and relax most of Saturday afternoon, except for cooking, and then Sunday is a true day of rest for me. It is so relaxing! We go to church, visit friends, sometimes go to a park and have some fun there, or have company over to our place.

When I was a little girl, I had to clean and cook and do tons of work, but the house was never clean. I was sweeping a dirt floor, sometimes sprinkling water on it to try and keep some of the dust down in the dry season. I was cooking inside the house with a wood fire, so of course there was nothing but smoke and grime. We washed our clothes in the river, but the river wasn't like the county swimming pool—clear and clean with chlorine in it. It was muddy brown, and nothing was ever truly clean. It was endless and sad. Can you imagine being here, in a nice apartment, how fun it is for me to keep house? It's the funnest thing I know.

Knitting

Even though I'm old enough to go to my Maker, I still like to feel useful, so I was happy to find this group of ladies who volunteer-knit. We make baby clothes, for babies who are hurt or lost or have to be taken from their mothers. We knit for premature babies, also. Blankets and tiny sweaters and hats, booties and mittens.

I have been knitting all my life, and that's a long time, ha ha. Well, but really now, eighty-four years is no joke. I have a lot of experience. I can make a good pair of booties in just one knitting session, and I mean good booties. Not the tube ones. No, the real ones where you have to turn and shape the heel so they don't get kicked off all the time. These booties are like real socks, and they have pretty patterns like lace or cables. Sometimes I make the tiniest of pom-poms to hang on them, so cute!

My son found this group for me. He knows I'm lonely, with him at work all day. Some of his friends said I should watch television, but I don't understand enough English; it just doesn't mean anything to me. I wish I had learned it when I was younger. I'm understanding more and more, but it sure is hard to make my stiff old tongue go around all those new sounds.

This knitting group, it meets once a week. One of the ladies picks me up and drops me off so I don't have to take the bus. They are all very nice to me, and they compliment me on my knitting. I am by far the fastest knitter they have. From them, I learned the phrase, "Good job!"

Sometimes I feel a little impatient with the slower ones. I know it's none of my business, but I think some of the ladies just come out of boredom or to chat with the others. Sometimes I'll see one of the ladies knit a few rows, put their knitting down in their lap, and then just drink the tea, eat the cookies, and chat. And there are all those babies waiting for something nice. Something that's not ragged or dirty, but pure and clean, like a prayer.

The man who comes to get the knitted items, he says they are really grateful for our work. He says the babies, some of them, come into the hospital with nothing nice at all. My hat or booties or little sweater set with matching shorts, that might be the only nice thing that baby had ever worn. The only thing of beauty. The only thing handmade by caring hands.

It's nice to sit with a group of ladies, even if they don't knit so fast. I just wish I could speak enough English to talk with them. That would be a lot more fun. But you can't have everything; I learned that a long time ago. At least the babies are getting something, bless them. And it's nice to feel like I can contribute something, even if I am old and ill. I'm not dead yet!

Las Malvinas

I understand everything the doctor is telling me. The reason I asked for an interpreter is that I took an oath to no longer allow a word of English to pass my lips, in honor of our dead boys who were left to rot in Las Malvinas. No, they are not the Falkland Islands; they are Las Malvinas, and they belong to my country, Argentina!

What business do the British have poking their noses around and grabbing onto territory around the world in this day and age, anyway? We are a civilized nation! Do they think it is still the 1800s and they can run around the world with their round safari hats and their umbrellas and their high teas and colonize everyone? It's an outrage!

Our boys, our own Argentinean soldiers, young recruits, the land's finest young men, they laid down their lives to defend a tiny piece of our territory, our national pride, and our national heritage. The Brits just flew over in their planes and bombed the island, killing our soldiers so they wouldn't have to face them in combat. Face-to-face would have been different.

Who are the English, after all, to fly to our land, our country, and start claiming a piece of it? Do you think for a moment that if they flew to Hawaii and started bombing it, this country would not fight? Of course they would; it goes without saying! Look what happened when Japan bombed Pearl Harbor! The United States dropped nuclear bombs on two major cities, killing countless civilians! The English only do this knowing they can get away with it, but although we don't have the military power to bomb them back, Argentina will never forget.

Once the skirmishes were over, and Argentina had lost and was forced to cede the territory to foreign occupation, our president formally requested that we be allowed to land on the island and recover our dead. Can you imagine? The British get to keep the island; we just want the bodies of our fallen soldiers, our young men, to return them to their families. And the British said no! They left the boys, our boys, to rot in the snow, like animal carcasses, like dead seals on the beach. These are human beings, for God's sake, not animals.

What possible purpose could the British have for doing this except to humiliate and attempt to dehumanize us? But they can't take away our humanity! We have a nation; we have a culture; we have a language, and neither their bombs nor their body snatching will stop me from speaking my language and rejecting theirs! So you don't need to interpret what the doctor says into Spanish for me, but just interpret my words into English, please. I shall not speak English again. I took an oath never to forget, and I shall not forget Las Malvinas.

Last Time

T his is the last time I come to this hospital. I mean, they didn't give him any-thing! And they made us wait for two hours in the emergency room wait-ing area. I don't know why they can't see how sick he is. Maybe he looks good to them; God knows what they see in this hospital that might harden their hearts to a mother's suffering. But my son really is ill. I am his mother; I know him, and I know how ill he really is. Believe me, I would not be sitting in a hos-pital emergency room for no reason at all.

He has been throwing up for a week. He won't eat any solid foods, and if I make him, he throws it up! Then the doctor goes and says that's good! He said the baby knows he should just have liquids, and as long as he has enough milk and juice, he will be okay. That's easy for the doctor to say; he isn't a mother. You can't live on liquids alone, once you are used to real food.

I asked the doctor, I said, I think my son is in a weakened state. My friend, she went to this other clinic, and they gave her son these drops to put in his milk, and right away his color came back, his appetite, his strength, everything! But this doctor, he doesn't care. He says probably that other baby had anemia and mine doesn't; mine just has a flu. He won't give me anything, not even vitamin drops. Not even Tylenol! He says it's not a prescription drug.

I would never have taken the time to get all the way over here and come to the emergency room if I knew the doctor wasn't going to do anything. I should have just stayed home. My husband is the one who pressured me. He said, what if our baby has something horrible, like cancer or tuberculosis? Are you just go-ing to sit around the house for days or weeks watching him get sicker until he dies? For God's sake, woman, take him to the clinic.

I called the clinic, but they have this thing where they think I take him in too much, and I know the receptionist doesn't like me. She asked about all the symp-toms herself instead of letting me talk to the doctor or nurse. She said they were too busy to talk to me. But how could they be too busy to help a sick child? Isn't that their only job? Then she said they were booked up, and I couldn't come in for three days. That's why I came here, but I'll never come here again.

It's not easy being a mother in a foreign place, and you don't have your mother to help you and you don't have any aunties and you don't even have any older sis-ters with their babies to scold you and give you good advice. People joke about not wanting their mother-in-law's advice, but I would even be happy with her nearby. The doctor acts like I'm stupid and naïve, but how would I know if my son just has a flu, or something horrible? I have no one.

Laughter

You know that saying that you laugh so you won't cry? I'm like that. I'm joking around all the time. When I found out I had this heart condition, they said they were going to do a special X-ray, like a scan, and they would see what was inside of me without cutting me open. So after the study, my sister called me and she said, well, sister, what did they find?

Death, I told her.

What? What are you talking about? she told me.

Death; they looked inside my skeleton, and they found death inside of me.

Before she got really upset, I told her I was just kidding; they just found this thing with my heart, and they think they can fix it. She got mad and relieved at the same time and said, little sister, how can you still be joking around at a time like this? But you know, you laugh so you don't cry! How would it help my heart if I sat around crying about it? Better to laugh.

My husband, he is very modest and strict. He asks me, why are you such a simple person? You tell everyone your personal business. Why are you so open? But that's how I am. Like today, he was just sitting, saying nothing, like he always does, and then the nurse said, take everything off the top for the cardiologist to examine you, but you can leave your bra on. And I turned kind of slyly to my husband and said, uh-oh. But I'm not wearing a bra today! Well, his quiet little head in his pulled-down baseball cap swiveled around like a shot, and he just stared at me aghast until I pulled my shirt up and showed him I was just pulling his leg. He is so quiet, sometimes at home I'll just talk for hours, and then I'll say, okay, I'm done, now it's your turn, and he'll just say his head is empty and he has nothing to add. He likes to listen. Luckily!

Then just now, when they were shaving me for the procedure, I saw they shaved me down both sides by the thighs, but left a strip of hair in the middle, and I told you to tell the nurse I don't care too much for my new hairstyle, and we joked about maybe I can tell my husband it's the latest style among city women. That's the kind of thing that keeps me going; I mean, I'm all nervous about this long catheter going into my groin and all the way to my heart to burn off that extra flap of tissue, and yet I'm lying here amused thinking about my new pubic hairstyle. I can't wait to tell my husband about the joke; it's funny.

I think it's a real gift to find humor in things, to talk openly with people, to make friends easily. It's the only way to get through this vale of tears. Nah, just kidding! What vale of tears? Life is good. As long as you can still laugh, there is still life in you. Laughter means hope.

Leukemia

A guy doesn't come here to complain; he comes here to work. So when I sent for my eighteen-year-old nephew so he could earn some money and send it back home, he came and he worked and he didn't complain. But now I have to wonder: how long was he in pain and just never told us? He's what we call a gentle soul, just a real quiet type.

He started getting bruises more easily, but so what? A lot of us who work two jobs bruise easily because our blood gets weak from not enough sleep and bad food, since our wives are all back home. We eat from cans and wash our own clothes. My nephew, he's only working one job, so I didn't think it was too much for him. His hip hurt real bad, but he hadn't fallen down or anything. Then his gums started bleeding. He seemed kind of embarrassed to tell us about it, but it was clear he was hurting really bad. We took him to a hospital and they transferred him here, and now out of the blue, it's leukemia. From one minute to the next. Leukemia!

He just found out an hour ago, and the doctor basically said, hey, you can start chemotherapy tonight, or you can die. That's it. Now, what do you want to do? My nephew, he keeps playing with his IV line, making little knots in it and then untying it, like a nervous girl will play with her hair, you know. Not that he's ever known a young girl like that; he's just worked to help his family since he was a little kid, with no time to spare for his own fun. He's still just a little kid. When the doctor left, he just looked at me and said, Uncle, what can I do?

I don't know what to tell him. I didn't bring him here to die, I know that for sure. I don't know what my brother and sister-in-law are going to have to say to me about it. Like, why didn't I take care of him? Why didn't I know? Why did he have to get sick here of all places where he can be caught and deported in the middle of treatment?

The hard thing is, I'm his uncle. I'm his elder. I'm like his father here. He looks to me for answers. I'm supposed to know things. And I don't have any answers. Back in the old country, we like to say, God's will be done. These are mysteries beyond our understanding. But now I've been here for a long time, long enough to learn English and get my green card, and I don't believe in that stuff anymore. I don't think that way, and I want to punch someone in the face and ask God to tell me what is going on here. I don't want my nephew to die of leukemia when he hasn't had a chance at anything. All my nephew has ever done is work his ass off to help others. And yet this country is filled with young people, just his age, who have never worked a day in their life. What about my nephew? Why can't he have a turn at this life?

Lie

I knew I didn't feel that attracted to women in high school, but I didn't know much more than that. I was pretty innocent. So I just didn't date and concentrated on my studies. When I went to college, I was in a bigger city. One of the first people I met was this one guy. He was skinny and a little unhealthy. He said he had always been sickly with allergies and asthma.

This twenty-eight-year-old graduate student, he pursued a friendship with me from day one. It's like he somehow knew I was gay even before I did. He sensed it. We didn't talk about it yet. But we spent a lot of time together. I started going to his place, and since he had his own room in a student house, we would mostly hang out in his room and listen to music.

One night, about four months after we met, when he was already my best friend in the world and knew everything about me, he asked me to come over and drink with him. He had rented some movies and had the lights low so we could watch the television screen. We watched some movie about something while we drank, and then he had a movie about men in Mexico City. And they were gay and being interviewed about how they felt. And what they said was just what I felt. That blew me away. I didn't know, didn't realize that anyone else felt like me.

I had drunk quite a bit, and I started to cry. I told my friend, I never knew other people felt like me, and he said, listen, I feel like you. I feel like you. And he took me in his arms, and he made love to me, and I let him. After that, we were lovers for three months, then he got sicker, and he broke up with me and moved back to his part of the country. He gave me his address, but he told me not to write unless I really needed to. He needed to be alone, he told me.

Years later, I moved to the U.S. and found this man, a really good, kind man. This man told me that couples always get checked for HIV before they get together. And it turned out he was negative, and I was positive. And now he is so cautious, he doesn't even want to kiss me. And it hurts. And what hurts more is, I've only slept with one man in my life and it's over.

I gathered up the courage to write the guy in Mexico, the guy who seduced me when I was eighteen, and ask him if he knew. It was so hard to write that letter. I crumpled up so many versions of it. When I finally sent the letter, it came back to me, marked deceased. I was left with the letter in my hand, hating him, so angry, and no one left to be angry at. I wish I could talk to him and find out why he lied. I loved him and thought he loved me, too. He must have known he was sick, but I wanted him to say it. I wanted him to admit that he took advantage of me and took away my ability to give and receive love freely.

Living Will

L ooks like I have everything ready for my gallbladder surgery, then. One more question? You want to ask me about a living will? No, I don't have any will at all. What is a living will?

It tells you what my wishes are if I can no longer speak on my own behalf, like if I have a stroke, or become paralyzed, or get brain damage during surgery. Oh, I see. Just in case anything goes wrong with the surgery. Hmm.

Look, is there something you're not telling me about the surgery? I thought the doctor said it was a safe, easy procedure. Does he think I might become unable to speak on my own behalf?

So you're saying I'm safe. But just in case, I should write down who will decide about my future, like whether to unplug me, if I am no longer able to talk or think for myself. And I should also decide if I want to—give my organs away?!

Just a minute, now. I think there must be some mistake. The doctor said this was a safe procedure, didn't he? But now that I think about it, he did make me sign a document saying that I understood there could be bleeding, infection, or damage to surrounding organs. And the anesthesia guy said that every once in a while, someone dies from the anesthesia.

I have to stop and think. I wasn't prepared for all this. I thought I was just having a simple surgery. I mean, I've been in a lot of pain, but it's not worth dying over. It's not worth being cut up and having pieces of me given away to other people. I think I might just rather keep having the gallbladder pain. I read in my country about some patients dying "accidentally on purpose," and then the hospital used their organs. Is it too late to back out of the surgery now?

What do you mean you don't care if I fill this living will out, that you have to ask everyone by law? Are you saying I don't need a living will, or I do need one? You think I should have one just in case? Just in case what, though? That's my question. Just tell me straight up: Does the doctor think he's going to kill me during surgery, because I think I have a right to know. I'd rather just know up front, so I can make plans and say my goodbyes.

Now you say you don't care if I have a living will? But you are the one who said it would be a good idea, didn't you? Oh, you're supposed to say it's a good idea, so more people will have them, because then the hospital won't have to decide what to do with people. Well, if you want to know what to do with me, all you have to do is take out my gallbladder and send me home. And I'll warn you up front: I'm not signing a living will, and you can't keep my organs.

Low Class

It is so hard to adjust to being in this country. There is such a different mix of people. Maybe it's because all of a sudden, just by moving here, I have become a member of the lower classes. I am now one of the poor, and that means I am going to associate with uneducated people, many of whom are from the countryside of their respective countries. At least that is how I make sense of the fact that I have ended up with the lover I have, a Mexican peasant.

He is physically gorgeous, very nicely shaped, and muscular. He has large, soulful eyes and a nice, bristly moustache to rub me with. He is an adventuresome lover, ever eager and manly, eight years younger than I am. He thinks I'm beautiful; he tells me I am. But he is so low class! I would be embarrassed to have anyone find out I am with him. If I ever had any visitors from home, they could never, ever meet him!

Take this example. Now, I am a woman for whom hygiene is paramount. I like to be squeaky clean from head to toe. When I was going to meet my lover, had consented to go to his home for the first time, he knew I was planning to give myself to him. I prepared myself fully. I washed and dried my hair; I scrubbed myself head to toe; I powdered and perfumed myself; and I finished off with very nice clothes and makeup. When I got to his home, he had asked all his roommates to leave. He was excited and nervous. So was I. We stood and kissed.

Then he invited me to the couch. He had music on, ranch music, but what can you do? He likes it. He started to stroke me, then he said, honey, why don't you go take a shower?

Go take a shower! Can you believe it? He thought I was dirty. He was bathed, but he didn't realize I would know enough to clean myself before making love; he thought he had to tell me to bathe. I came close to walking out, but instead, I calmly told him, my dear, I am already bathed and cleaned, and he said, oh, I didn't know.

Then he went further in earnest, and he started sucking my neck and leaving large marks on it, and I asked him what are you doing? People will see these marks, these hickeys. And he laughed and said, I know. I want them to. I want everyone to know that you belong to me. Well, I've been very lonely in this country, and I've continued to see him. But I still wonder how it would be if I found a man from my own country, an educated man. I can't help remembering a certain man from my home country, my first lover. Kind, educated, gentle, polished, sophisticated—he never asked if I had bathed. Pure class! He was everything to me. How I loved him! He had only one defect: He was married. Aside from that, he was perfect.

Luck

There are different kinds of luck, you know. Some people think lucky means you get every little thing just like you want it, but that's not true. God controls your luck, and He may not want you to have every little thing, because it might not be best for your soul. Just like a parent doesn't want their child to be spoiled rotten. A parent wants the child to be good.

Take me; I'm lucky. You know I've had this brain tumor, and they did surgery. Boy, was that interesting! I have friends that had that cataract thing, what do you call it, laser surgery? And they got a video of it to show their friends. I asked the doctor, you're going to open up the roof of my mouth and reach into my brain to take the tumor out—can I get a film of it to show my friends? I never met anyone who got to see their own brain before, not even on film.

The doctor said no, you wouldn't want to see it. Then he said it would be a disturbance to have a camera there. He said it wasn't like eye surgery. Anyway, now they're going to consider surgery again, since the brain tumor came back. But that's not what I mean about luck.

What I mean about luck is this: Five years ago, I was walking across the street from the hotel where I worked in housekeeping, and I was hit by a bus. He didn't see me, of course, and he broke my leg in a bunch of places; they called it a multiple fracture. It hurt so bad! I kept praying, now God, Dear, why did you have to let that happen to me? What is Your plan? I am in so much pain! How could this help me? I tried to be polite about it, but I was a little ticked.

Well, like most prayers, I didn't get an answer right away. What is time to God? Then when I found out about the brain tumor, I got my answer. You see, I used to be a rushing, sort of impatient person. Always hurrying, very efficient, and no time to waste. After my leg was hurt, I had to slow down. I developed something I never had before: incredible patience.

Now with the brain cancer, you wouldn't believe what I have been through. The pain, the studies, the operations, the recovery, the pain, the pain, the pain! But guess what? God gave me a secret weapon! Patience! I never would have had that gift to use now, to alleviate my suffering to such a degree, unless God let that bus hit me like He did.

Now the doctors tell me, you are the most patient lady we have ever treated. I just smile and tell them, God works in mysterious ways. If one of them ever has the time to listen, I might tell them how I got so patient. Who ever thought I'd be praying and praising God for hitting me with a metro bus? But I am. I really am grateful to have all this useful patience. Thank God!

Maid

People don't realize how hard it is to work as a hotel maid. It is depressing. To clean the same hotel rooms over and over every day without any change, to rush from room to room in a sweat in your polyester uniform, flying down the hall with your cart of supplies, flipping those heavy mattresses and moving the furniture, climbing up on sink counters to wash the tops of the mirrors with harsh chemicals, gathering dirty linens—that's a hard, hard and lonely life.

The loneliness! You have no idea how lonely it can be. We have no coworkers to speak of; we have to do everything alone. If we are even seen stopping to tell another maid something by the elevator, we get in big trouble. They have security cameras everywhere, and they have strict rules about us not talking to each other. So when I get to my floor, I get out of the elevator with my cart and look down that long, empty hall, and I'm all alone. There is no one anywhere; all the visitors have checked out, all the rooms have their remains of leftover coffee, soiled linens, damp towels on the floor, garbage from the food they brought in. And the dirty, unmade beds. Who knows who's been in them? And I have to go pick it all up, even though it's going to look just like that when I arrive to clean tomorrow.

And now we have to rush faster and faster, because of the excuse of the bad economy. Somehow, that means we have to clean eighteen or nineteen rooms a day instead of twelve or thirteen. For the same pay, yet we are supposed to get the rooms just as clean in less time. It is so stressful! Run, run, run. We have a half-hour lunch. We're not allowed to eat in the hotel rooms, only the break room. And we can't leave our carts out. By the time we store our carts and get downstairs, we've lost half our lunch break. So we have to try to wolf something down in a couple of minutes and rush back to work. It is impossible to eat in ten minutes and then return to running from room to room, pushing a vacuum around, scrubbing mirrors and tile, turning over the mattresses and remaking the beds, lifting and moving—you'd end up throwing up. So most of us just don't eat all day. I don't eat all day.

I've been here a long time. I'd like to find a better job, but I don't speak enough English. I thought I would learn it at work, but I didn't realize I wouldn't ever talk to anyone at work, so I have no chance to learn it. Sometimes I get off the elevator and start pushing my cart down the long, empty hall, and I just have to blink back the tears. Sorry to complain; I don't mean to. I try to be strong and brave, but I just didn't think it would be like this to live in the United States. Maybe I'm naïve, but I thought if I worked hard, after a while, I could get ahead.

Memory

The social worker means well. I am sure of that. She even told me about her own loss, in her own family. But I think she just doesn't understand what I'm going through when she gives me this advice, about holding his memory. Trying to keep him alive. Thinking about him and talking about him all the time. Maybe it's different when you lose a child. I don't know. This was my brother. My baby brother.

I know it's only been a couple months, but I don't have that problem of forgetting him. I just keep feeling his presence all the time, and I wish it would let up. Yesterday, I came out into the living room when I woke up, and I saw his bike by the door and was wondering if he was going to be late for work, and then I remembered he's dead. He's not going to work anymore. And I felt this huge wave of grief pouring over me, and I had to just stand there and stare at the bike for about ten minutes, blinking to hold back the tears.

Then I went to sit on the sofa, but my wife had laundry stacked on it, so I went to sit in the rocker and I saw it moving, probably from my movement, but I remember exactly how my brother used to sit there with my kids climbing all over him, calling Uncle, Uncle, trying to get his attention and trying to be the one on his lap, while he would laugh and tell them to take turns. They loved him so much. We all lived together, and they would run and hug him when he came to the door. He was young; he didn't have his own family yet. We were his family.

We had a picture of him on the living room wall, but I took it down. I felt like he kept following me with his eyes. See, he is a lot younger than me, and when we were little, he used to always want to come everywhere with me, but he knew I didn't like him to always be pestering me. So a lot of times, he would just follow me with his eyes while I was getting ready to go somewhere, and then I would know he really wanted to come, and I would tell him, okay, you can come, and his whole face would light up, and he would run and get ready.

He would follow me everywhere, and he followed me to the United States, and now he's dead. I dream about him every night; I am afraid to fall asleep. I don't know how to get him out of my head. I keep thinking he's following me with his eyes, asking me to take care of him, asking me to do things for him, and now there is no way I can ever do anything for him again. He is beyond my reach, and I don't know where he is, and I can never, ever help him with anything again. He's my little brother and I'm supposed to help him, but I can't. The social worker says I can still love him, but my job was to do for him, and I can never do for him again.

Men Doctors

I can't believe I had to go through that! I have never, ever had a man doctor, and now I had to have two of them at the same time! It's bad enough I am here pregnant, stuck on bed rest for high blood pressure, and now they are telling me my labor is not going to progress, and I probably need a Cesarean. On top of all that, they have to send me two young men doctors to poke around in my private parts. Lord, have mercy.

That curly-haired one, the pasty pale-white one, he was in there last night poking around; that's why I said I didn't want them today. He hurt me really bad. He just doesn't know what he is doing, and he dug around like he thought he'd find something new in there. I know they have to train doctors, but couldn't they find an easier case? Like a low-risk birth with someone who is used to men doctors, maybe? I mean, why do they have to use me?

Besides, why are there two of them? They remind me of those Mormon missionaries that come through my country, always in pairs and always young and serious, and they don't know how to talk to people and they know better than you and then they wonder why nobody wants their God. And they both put gloves on, and they both stand down where they can look at my private parts as I am supposed to spread open. Why does the one guy have to look at me while the other guy checks? Can't he at least stand to the side or look the other way or something?

All this while, they are saying relax. Relax! Sure! And put your heels together and shove them all the way up against your buttocks while you're nine months pregnant, and just relax. Then do everything they say and drop the knees wide open, while the men—oh, my God!

Then when I asked to have the woman doctor check me instead, the one man doctor, the nervous one, he comes and tells me it is important to have the same two men doctors check me so they can see whether there has been any change, any progress in the labor. That will help them to decide, he told me, if they are going to have to do a Cesarean.

And now after all those vaginal exams last night and overnight and today and then again this afternoon, these two men doctors, they come in and tell me they are off the case. And now that I have the surgery team doctors, the obstetricians— who are all women—I am going to have a Cesarean. After four days of asking, I finally get the women doctors, but it's too late.

I can't help but wonder if I could have had a vaginal birth if I had had the women doctors all along. Then I could have relaxed. My legs just trembled every time those men doctors came near me. I mean, if I could have relaxed, could I have opened up? Now I'll never know.

Miniskirt

en are strange. I don't say it to complain; I'm just stating a fact. Take my boyfriend. He is jealous in a lot of ways, yet he wants me, he begs me, he orders me to dress sexy. He loves to take me shopping, and he wants me to buy things like lacy underwear and miniskirts. And not just for his private pleasure; he expects me to dress like this in public. I don't know what he is thinking. I don't know why he would like that. I think it's just bizarre.

He actually told me, he wants other men to desire me. He thinks it is exciting and fun and something that gives him pride, to say, look at this, this is all mine and you can't have it, but I bet you want it, and I bet you wonder how I got it, and how I can keep it. That is pretty much what he tried to explain to me about it. But I still think it's strange.

See, what I want my girlfriends to see is not just some handsome man; I want them to see that I have a decent, honest, and hardworking man. A man who is tender and solicitous of my needs and drives me places and is kind to my family and wants to get a good job and take care of me and maybe marry me and have children. That is the kind of man I would show off, not a man who looks nice in a certain pair of pants. The whole idea is just laughable, to a woman.

So I have a hard time understanding, and I asked him, don't you want your friends to think I am a decent, loving, kind, and good woman? And he laughed and said, not really. What is going to impress my friends is if I have someone like you, someone who is taller than me and gorgeous and has legs up to there and beautiful, chocolaty skin and paints her nails and knows how to wear makeup and dress well. They can't stand it; it eats them up. It kills them!

I can't believe you are telling me this, I told him. Your friends don't even care if I am a good person, the kind of woman who would make a good wife; they don't even care if I would be a good mother? Your friends don't even care if I'm decent?

Why would they, he told me, they don't want to marry you; they just want to look at you.

Then when he saw how upset I was, he told me he loves me, he cares a lot about what kind of a person I am, he knows how good and kind and decent and hardworking I am, and it matters a lot to him, and if it bothers me to dress up for his friends, then I don't have to do it and he will still love me. But next thing I know, he is pulling a lacy bra and a miniskirt out of my closet and holding them up with a big, stupid grin on his face and waving them back and forth with a questioning look, like, I'm know I'm an idiot, but could you please wear these anyway?

That's why I'm saying, I'm not complaining, but men are really strange. Really.

Miracle

D octor, you have wrought a miracle in my life, and I will never, ever tire of praying for you and for all your people and for God to allow you to keep your health and be able to continue working as a doctor and carrying out your professional duties for the benefit of other patients.

You must know that I spent fifteen years nearly blind, and I had never dreamed there was this cataract surgery to fix it. When it first started to happen, I went to the clinic for farmworkers, and they said it was a special disease that had to get really bad before you could do anything; they said something like the cataracts had to get ripe or mature. So they just kept telling me that, and finally I gave up and quit going. I just figured I would end up being blind.

Then my children kept after me to see a specialist, all the time, until I gave in and came here, and now look! Here I am, looking at you as clear as day! And doctor, let me hold your hand for a moment and tell you, I honestly do pray for you every single night before I lay me down to sleep. Let me tell you, God will not forget you, because I am here to remind Him in case He gets too busy to remember you on His own. I just added you to the people I already pray for, so it's no bother at all. Really.

This is what I say in my nightly prayer. Dear Blessed Lord, please remember to care for the gentle doctor who has restored my eyesight and allowed me to see my grandchildren, who before this were just blurs of light to me. Please, oh Lord, guide his hands so he can carefully operate on others like me so they, too, can see. Please protect his health and allow him to continue forward in his sacred healing work with your guidance and protection. And Lord, this doctor does so much for others; please bring him some peace and happiness in his home life as well, allowing him to enjoy the fruits of his labor surrounded by his loved ones. Keep him strong to continue Your work, Dear Lord, and keep his hand steady. This I pray.

Well, doctor, if there is anything else you need me to pray for, you let me know at the next checkup, because like I told you, I will never tire of praying for you or calling down blessings upon your head, because you have indeed wrought a miracle in my life and the life of my family. If regaining my eyesight isn't a miracle, then I don't know what is. This is what they talk about in the Bible, doctor. The ones who couldn't walk regained their legs. The blind ones regained their sight, just like me. It's a miracle. I can see! I can see again, doctor! I was blind, and I can see. So may God just keep on blessing you and your gift of sight. You are truly a miracle worker, and that lets me know that God loves you indeed.

Mitten

We're here from Sunnyside, and my mom has cancer. She had appointments all day today, and now tomorrow she has surgery. Poor thing, she's never even had a tooth pulled in all her livelong days, have you, Mom? No, she hasn't. That's why four of us came with her; this is my dad, my sister, my sister's husband, and me, her son. This is just the delegation, you know; the rest of them are waiting at home. Each of the four of us had to come to help Mom, you see.

Anyway, they told us that we can get a hotel for the nights she has to be in town, but now that the day is gone and it's dark out and too late to drive back to Sunnyside and get back here in the morning, the social worker just mentioned that only one person is allowed to stay in the hotel room with my mom. I'm afraid that's going to be a big problem for us, since there are five of us.

You see, I'm her son, and I'm the best driver for snow. My dad, well, he has to be with his beloved bride, after all their years together. He's not going to consent to sit home alone in Sunnyside, knowing my mom is over here in this big, huge city all by herself. So he had to be here. My sister, now, she's the one with the gentle touch. She's Mom's favorite child, so she'll be the one taking care of Mom and staying in her hospital room after surgery; she just can't leave Mom at all. Then my sister's husband, he's the one who has been to Seattle a lot; he knew where this hospital was, you see, so we never could have found the hospital without his guidance. They say there are eight hospitals just in Seattle, and even more in other cities around here, so we could have spent weeks trying to find the right one. They sent us a map, but you know maps aren't that easy to read, especially in English.

Basically, I think you can see that we took the minimum number of people here to get the job done. There really isn't anyone we could have left behind, see. So I'm thinking, maybe if you, since you speak English, could please call the hotel on our behalf and kind of explain, well, it's kind of like this. Since we drive over the pass, we see people wearing gloves and mittens, right? And gloves, that's like seeing us as five people, and if you look at it that way, we can't get the hotel room. But if you look at it another way, we're more like five fingers inside a mitten, and a mitten is like one thing, you know? One, not five. So maybe if you talk to them at the hotel and explain things a little in English, they could understand; we're just kind of like five fingers all warm and cozy and snug together in a mitten, but we are inseparable. So could we please all stay in the hotel room together? That way we can all stay with Mom. Please. It's just that most people here are more like a glove, and we're more like a mitten, you understand?

Mom

My husband says I'm a baby because I miss my mom. I cry for her almost every night. I was never away from her in my life, and this separation is horrible. He came to my country to work, and that's how we met. He already spoke Spanish, and he was very respectful to my family. He came and asked them if he could go out with me, even though they are poor. They couldn't believe someone like him, tall and white and educated, would be interested in me, and they used to tease me about it. They didn't expect it to go anywhere, since he was just visiting.

Then his job ended, and he asked to marry me and move me here, to Seattle. I had very mixed feelings, because I'd never known a man like him or even met anyone like him before. I was in love with him and took the chance for a better life. But here I am, I don't know anyone, and I am so lonely! He is gone all the time at work, and the day lasts so long.

He is pushing me to learn English right away and tries to have me speak English even with him. He wants me to be able to talk with his family. He said my mom is your mom now, and you have to learn English so you can speak to your new mom. But it's so hard for me!

He gets really mad at me about my mom. He told me I'm immature, because it's not normal for someone to love their parents that much, to be that attached. He said he's traveled many years since he was young, and he doesn't cry for his family. He's mature and independent. He wants me to grow up, too, to be more individual, not to be such a big baby all the time.

But I can't help thinking about my mother. I told my mom, if I marry this man, I can send you money and you won't have to work so hard for my brothers and sisters. I'm the oldest child. I was working to give the money to my parents, and now I can't work because I have a baby and he doesn't want me to work. He doesn't want to send them money every month because things are tight. He said we can't afford it, and they are not good parents if they expect me to support them. His parents don't need anything from him, but then, they are here, not in my country.

I dream a lot about my home. In my dreams, all the flowers and even the air and sky look and smell just like I remember, and my house is there and my whole family. I dream about my mom a lot, and she is always hugging me and stroking my hair like she used to and telling me she loves me, and I am home again and living with them, and I'm not married and I don't have a baby, but then my mom is always crying in this dream and so am I, and I start wondering why we are sad. And then I always wake up and remember. I try not to miss my mom because it makes him mad, but I still do miss her. I stay busy all day, but the night won't let me forget her.

Money

Everybody seems to want to move up, get ahead, make more and more money. But me, I don't have these illusions. I don't want to end up with more money. I know the problems that pride and greed and vanity bring to a family. Take my husband, for example. We worked side by side in the field in our country. We didn't argue about money; we just shared the burden and worked side by side, poor as we were. We never fought about anything, before.

As soon as we got here, everything changed. He went out to work and took English classes, and I stayed home. He makes enough money to support us, but now he insists that I work full-time instead of taking English classes. He's one of these men who want to move up, but keep the woman down. So I have to work as well, even though we have two children. I have to spend ten hours a day away from my kids, just to get him more money.

My husband, he wants to be the big man now. He sees that I can bring home almost five hundred dollars twice a month, and that's a handy sum. He isn't thinking about the best interest of the children anymore, about having a happy home. I told him, you're a man. It's your job to provide for your family, and I have two hands and I'm honest and I don't mind pitching in, but believe me, I do not agree to just work more and more so you can act like a big man and loan money to your friends. Which he has done.

He has changed so much since we left the farm. He is making twelve dollars an hour now and has become so self-important. He bought a truck we have to pay three hundred dollars a month for, and he says it's a good truck. I told him, a good truck is not a truck that takes you and your friends out and about, while I sit at home worried sick about what you are doing, who you are with. What's wrong with the bus? Is this what we are working so hard for, so you can run around? Money doesn't impress me. Honesty and decency and hard work impress me.

If you saw him, you would laugh; he has become just that vain. Can you imagine him on the farm with gold chains hanging off his neck? Wearing aftershave and hair gel? He looks ridiculous. It's all about him now; he's the big man about town, the man with the money and the friends and the truck and the clothes. He throws money away on his friends. But that's the problem with money. It seems like everything was easier when we didn't have any. I know we need money to live, but the extra money makes a person greedy and selfish and vain. My husband is a perfect example of that. There's a reason why the Bible says that money is the root of all evil. There's real wisdom in that saying. So no. I, for one, don't want more money.

Monopoly

T alk about monopoly. I went to Tijuana a while back. I filled up the tank in the United States, and it was eighteen dollars. I thought, that's a lot; I'll fill up in Mexico on the way back; everything's cheaper in Mexico since the peso dropped from three to a dollar to ten to a dollar. So on the way back, I filled up the tank in Tijuana. The guy said, that'll be 480 pesos, which is almost fifty dollars! I said, no way, that's crazy. He said, okay. You don't like it here at Pemex, you can go somewhere else. I said, I will next time. Where can I go? He says, two blocks that way, there's another gas station, Pemex. Or if you prefer, a couple miles up the highway, there's a Pemex station. If you don't like that, go down the river three miles, and there's another gas station: Pemex. Get it? It's nationalized. You don't like it? Go to Pemex!

Take my cell phone. I have Cingular Wireless. If I don't like it, I switch to Sprint, or MCI, or whatever. In Mexico, I bought a house. I called the phone company, Telmex, and asked to get the phone hooked up. They said okay, come in and sign a contract, and then we can install it and start services. But first, you have to sign a contract, a service contract.

So I went to the phone company office, and the lady said, sign this contract. I look at it, and it has a five thousand-peso hookup charge. I said, no way, I'm not going to pay five thousand pesos just to hook the phone up. I'll go somewhere else. She laughed and said, this is Telmex; everyone is Telmex. It's nationalized. You can go to another office, and they'll tell you the same thing. We're all Telmex. There is no one else. You have to pay it to have a phone in Mexico.

So I signed the contract and payed the amount, like five hundred dollars. So I said, okay, now when will the phone line be hooked up? The lady said, I'm sorry, I can't tell you that. What do you mean, I said? Well, it could be whenever they get time; we're really busy. Like when, I asked her? Like six months to a year; we're really, really busy, backlogged. You've got to be kidding, I told her. Who else can hook it up? Telmex, she said. Only Telmex. It's nationalized.

But that's not all! She said my contract says I pay the phone bill from the contract date, not the hookup date. So I have to pay the phone bill every month, for maybe a year, but I don't have a phone, because they haven't hooked it up. I couldn't believe it, but I asked around and that's really what they do! People pay their phone bill every month, but they don't have a phone, and if they don't pay the bill for the phone they don't have, they'll never get a phone, and if they do pay it, they still don't have a phone, but they'll get one someday, except they won't know when until it happens. So when people here whine about Microsoft, I just laugh at them.

Morphine

My wife, my wife is in the waiting room. Yes, we've been married forty-three years and have ten children. Yes, we get along well, me and my wife. But there is always temptation, like today for example, ha ha! Isn't there? Ha ha! Yes, with ten children, my wife kept me awfully busy working and trying to maintain a home, let me tell you. I grew old quickly with all that work, but thank God we're over the worst of it now. Yes, now I'm finally retired, thank God.

What? The nurse thinks I look thirty-five and not sixty-eight? Well, tell her that's too bad, because I wanted to look twenty-five! And while I'm at it, I'd like to feel twenty-five again and have a chance with the ladies again. Even if I do have ten children already.

Tell me, do you have any children? Only two? Ha ha. What's the matter, did you have a television? Ha ha. Oh, I think I see. You were avoiding… Well, some people do that. Careful timing and all that; it's not a sin. But seriously, though, you are a very gorgeous woman. Me, even with a television, I would not have been able to resist you. I'm only telling the truth.

How does your husband treat you? Has he made you suffer very much? Has he? I only ask because I wonder, how would you like to have a second husband as well? Maybe you would like two of us? What do you think? Eh? No? You think one is enough trouble? Well, ha ha! Maybe you're right! But listen, has your husband made you suffer very much? Because you don't look like you deserve that. You are a beautiful woman, and a very pleasant companion.

Tell the nurse, too, she is very attractive and so kindhearted! Is she married, too? Oh, she is! And she looks so fresh and young! Ha ha. Tell her that; see if I can make her blush. Tell her she looks young and untouched, ha ha! Tell her also, with the two of you at my side, one on each side of me, just like now, I think I could get an operation every day. Tell her that! Ask the nurse if I can come back tomorrow, ha ha! This is the best surgery I have ever had!

No, it's not the morphine talking, honestly; I've had surgery before! Really! I had a surgery in Guadalajara, and the nurse there, she was a despot! A regular dictator and meaner than sin. I tell you that my health declined rapidly based on her mistreatment of me. But here, I feel like I'm growing younger by the minute! I've never been treated better than this in my life!

You are so pretty. May I hold your hand? Well, may I hold the nurse's hand, then? Isn't it part of her job to keep me healthy? Ha ha! Tell the nurse, tell her that I might die of loneliness, and by holding my hand, she might save my life. Isn't it her job to keep me alive and healthy? Oh, well. Maybe my wife will do it later. Meanwhile, may I have a little more morphine?

Mother Mary

Yes, here he is, my premature baby. Nobody can believe that he made it, but he did, praise the Lord. Crawling and even starting to walk, just like any other child who lived nine months in his mother's womb. When you told me back then that I was going to have to have him at twenty-eight weeks, I didn't think he had a chance, no matter what the doctors said.

They gave me those shots of cortisone or whatever hormone it is that matures the baby's lungs, but come on. Twelve weeks left for God to knit the little bones together, put flesh on him, make his stomach and intestines and the rest of him. It's a little too much to ask that my baby would be so fine and healthy now. But nothing is too much for God. That is the absolute truth.

I went through a lot with this baby, and I think he senses it somehow. He is very affectionate with me, and when I hug him, he pats my back and shows me a lot of love. I can see in his eyes that he is grateful, and he loves me so much. He loves his mother.

As soon as I knew the bed rest wasn't going to work and I was going to have him early, from that period until I took him home from the hospital, I had a special prayer. I never told anyone about this, because I thought they might make fun of me, but I don't think you will make fun of me, since you also love babies so much and are a mother yourself.

I have been praying, well, not praying, I know that would be wrong, but I have been—well—asking Mother Mary to intercede with Jesus on my behalf. Now I know Mother Mary is just a woman, like you and me, but I got to thinking when I had all my mother worries, who better to pray to? Not pray to—she's not God, I know that—but who better to understand a mother's heart? So I thought, well, you have to pray to God or His holy son Jesus, of course, but then if Jesus is going to help me, don't you think He hears so many prayers every day? Don't you think if His Mother had heard something already about a certain little boy and a mother's suffering, and don't you think if His Mother wanted to talk to Him about it, well, don't you think He would lend her His ear? I mean, now, it is His own Mother, after all! Who would He be more likely to listen to than His own Mother Mary?

So I didn't pray to her, I knew that would be wrong, but I just asked her very politely if she could get her Son's attention, and then I prayed to Him for my son to be okay, and now he is, thank God. I'm not sacrilegious; I know she didn't heal my son, but I do think she helped, mother to mother. I know from personal experience that my son is more likely to listen to me than to anyone else, because I have done so much for him, and he is so grateful.

Mother's Day

I would have disowned my son, but my wife won't let me. You wouldn't believe what he did! He sent my wife flowers for Mother's Day. Sent from a shop! Didn't even bother to come by himself. Didn't even come by for one minute. You think a big bouquet would impress her? That's laughable! She is a mother! Then he called in the evening to see if she got the bouquet. What was he so busy doing that he couldn't come over in person? It was a Sunday!

I called my son, once I calmed down enough. I told him, son, you think your mother is going to be impressed with flowers? Let me tell you, since you seem to have forgotten. She carried you under her heart for nine months, son. She gave you life. She suckled you at her breast. She rocked you to sleep and cared for you all the days of your childhood. I wasn't around; I was busy working. She was the only one taking care of you.

Son, I told him, did your mother toss you out into a day-care center like these mothers do today? Did she just buy you expensive toys with the salary from her fun job to assuage her own guilt for not being present in your life? Why don't you answer? Is it because you're ashamed? You know the answer. You know she never did that to you. So why are you doing that to her? You think sending her flowers is anything but a humiliation to her? You're too important and busy on Mother's Day to see your own mother? What are you so busy doing?

Son, I told him, go out in your parking strip in front of your costly and elegant apartment complex. Pick a lawn daisy or a dandelion. Wrap it in a wet paper towel if you don't have a vase. And bring it over in person—you yourself—and hand it to your mother—you yourself—and kiss her on the cheek and thank her for what she has done for you. Acknowledge her sacrifice! Tell her you love her! Apologize for neglecting her! Who are you? Who are you to neglect her? You think the stork brought you? You wouldn't even be here without your mother.

And if you do come over—if you even bother to come over—she will decide if she will forgive you, with her mother's heart. She will turn the other cheek and make excuses for you, like she already has, but if it were up to me, son, I would disown you and throw you away right now, because as God is my witness, no son of mine would ever dare, EVER dare, to disrespect the woman who gave him birth and suckled him at her breast. No son of mine would dare! So you'd better get your butt over here and see what you can do to patch things up with your mom, but don't talk to me when you come, because you are not too big for me to put over my knee if I thought it would do you any good, and I might just be in the mood to do it, I told him.

Nun

I wanted to be a nun, but my knees were bad. You see, I grew up in a nice family in Peru. My parents were such good people, and they loved each other more than anything. We had a piano, and fresh-cut flowers at the dinner table every night, and good manners and kindness toward all. My parents set the example of loving-kindness, which we all followed.

Sometimes, when my father was out of town, my mother would tell us children, your father is a saint! Let's do something nice for your father! And we would set about cleaning up his den, shining and polishing everything, planting bulbs, or embroidering slippers for him.

My father, may he rest in peace, was just the same way. He never had a bad word to say about another human being. I never heard him swear. Never saw him raise his voice—let alone a hand—to anyone. He was a peaceful, joyous man. I only saw him get mad once, and that was when I told him I wanted to marry José. But he didn't yell at me, even then.

I went to Catholic school, and like I said, I always wanted to be a nun. But I have arthritis, and kneeling on those cold stone floors, well, even as a young girl, I just couldn't get back up. I sometimes wonder if the kneeling in the cold caused my arthritis, but I don't regret all that kneeling and praying; with all my sins, it will come in handy later on, ha ha!

At the Catholic school, there were several charity students. We tried to make them welcome, the poor girls from humble homes. One of my dear friends was from just such a home. Her mother was a widow. Her brother José was a charity student at a boys' school. I saw how he treated his mother and sisters, with so much love and protective kindness, and I admired him.

My father was very upset by José's proposal and refused to give his blessing or consent. He accused José of wanting to get some of our money. I was so in love, I gave up my parents to live with him. And like my father warned me, over time I regretted it. Oh, I didn't expect a piano and flowers on the table every evening. Just a kind, loving home with no raised voices.

Over the years, José grew very resentful and told me I was a bourgeois and should not have come down to marry him. He made a point of acting poorer than he was, swearing and being crude and vulgar. He also took up drinking after his mother died. I prayed for him to give up that vice, and God heard my prayers, but only after seventeen years. What is time to God, after all? Anyway, I love my children and my grandchildren, but sometimes I wonder what my life would have been if I had had good knees. How peaceful and restful it must feel to be a nun. Think about the peace and tranquility of being free to pray all day long, in peace!

Nurses

I just can't tell you how pleased I am with the nurses here in the United States. What a difference! When I had my first child, I thought I had died and gone to purgatory or below. There was wailing and gnashing of teeth! There were screams and slaps and lots of yelling. God protect me from ever giving birth in my part of Mexico again, let me tell you. The nurses here seem like angels to me, sent from heaven to be kind to us birthing mothers.

Where I was for my first birth, it was an open ward. Maybe a dozen skinny cots in a room. Lots of scared, young women—a couple as old as thirty or forty, having what they probably hoped was their last one—but mostly teenagers, like I was. One young one, maybe fifteen, couldn't hold it in. She started screaming with the pain. A nurse came up to her and slapped her, hard, across the face. She stopped screaming and held her cheek in shock. "You weren't crying when he was giving it to you, little Miss, so don't be coming around here crying now," the nurse told her, and the other nurses in the room started laughing.

That's what it was like the whole time. The nurses would not bring you a glass of water. They yelled at you if you vomited because it meant more work for them. A washcloth? Forget it. The only time you'd get attention would be if your baby was dying or they decided to do a Cesarean. Otherwise, you were on your own. They just yelled at someone to come cut the cord and plopped the baby on your belly. And our menfolk were not allowed anywhere near us.

Then I come here. They give me free childbirth classes. I get a hospital birth plan to fill out with what I want. My husband and even my sister can be in the room the whole time. They tell me I can bring my own music to play. They offer me water, three kinds of juice, coffee or tea, a heating pad or an ice pack, whatever I want. And the nurses keep coming in, asking, how are you? Are you feeling fine? Do you need anything? You're doing great! The baby's fine.

The first baby I had here was in California, and I was so shocked and relieved at the treatment that I started crying. The nurse came over and put a cold cloth on my forehead and started saying all kinds of soothing things and telling me everything would be okay. I didn't have enough language to tell her I was just so relieved and so happy about her nursing.

Now that I have an interpreter for this birth, I hope you will be able to let the nurses know how much I appreciate it. A birthing woman is very strong, but also vulnerable and sensitive. It makes a big difference to us to be treated extra kindly during the last few hours before we greet our new babies. It helps us to welcome them better. These nurses are truly changing lives.

Old Age

Yes, I'm an old woman now, and I do as I please. It wasn't always this way, believe me. I married at fifteen, and my husband was in his thirties. He certainly never dreamed he'd have a wife who talked back or made any decisions on her own, but that's what he has now! He's too old to beat me and his health won't permit him to drink, so he mostly stays in his room watching television and grumbling about everything.

Me, I watch my grandchildren almost every day. My favorite is my four-year-old. She minds me so well and helps me in the kitchen. She is very affectionate and just a cheerful little soul. She helps me also to prepare dinner. All of my daughters are educated and have good jobs. They work full-time and so do their young husbands, so they all come over to my home for dinner on weeknights. That way, they can eat a good, solid meal. I don't want them having fast food, since we have diabetes in our family. They could get sick quickly. And of course it's nice to have a family meal five times a week. It bonds the family together for when I'm gone.

My youngest son, he is single, and he takes me out almost every weekend. We don't drink alcohol, of course, and we don't go to dance clubs. But it seems that nearly every weekend, we are invited to a baptism, birthday party, coming-out party, wedding, or some other festivity, like a patron-saint celebration. My son and I love to dance, and we dance for hours at these parties. You know Latinos love dancing and music; that is no lie! I enjoy myself so much!

I used to invite my husband everywhere, but when he would go, he would get drunk, and we would have to leave. Then when he had to quit drinking, it made him nervous to be out and try to enjoy himself without alcohol, while others might be having a beer. Now, it's understood that I will go out while he stays home watching television.

Sure, sometimes I wish I could still pull him out of his bitterness and make him feel some of the joy that my life is to me. I pity him in his unhappiness, and as God is my witness, I have done everything I could in my power to make him a happy man, only nothing worked. He doesn't have it in him to be joyful, and he has always resented my joy.

He is like a mole in the light of my joy, and he just frowns and gets grumpy and wants me to turn it down, but I can't do that for him. I did it for so many years, talking quietly, trying not to laugh, never dancing, whispering in my own home like a thief in the night. Lonely. He had my youth—I gave him that—but he can't have my old age. Enough is enough. I must have joy.

Once

No one believes me, but I know you will. I have only had sex once in my life, and that was when I got pregnant, fifteen years ago. And I never would have done it like that, except I thought he was going to marry me. It's an old story, but it was new to me in my youth.

I was raised quite poor, even for my country's standards. My mother took in laundry, and my father was gone. My brothers and sisters left the house young to work, sometimes as live-in help in the city. That way, they got food and a uniform to wear and a place to sleep that was usually better than our house in the country. And running water and an inside toilet.

I never wanted to go to the city. I liked living in the country. When all my chores were done, my mother would let me go for walks, and I loved that. Sometimes, I would see this one boy, this one young man, whose family had so much more than we did, and he might follow me a step or two. Later on, he started meeting me on my walks, and he would accompany me.

I didn't want to get into any kind of trouble, because for a poor girl of humble birth, our decency was all we had to offer. We couldn't give that up lightly. But this young man, he spent a couple years pursuing me, even though his parents didn't approve of me. I'm not made of stone. I thought he really loved me. Can I tell you? Can I tell you how it happened?

One night, he told me he had something very important to tell me. He insisted that I meet him, said it could be life or death. I thought he might be ill or have to leave the country. Or his parents found out he wanted to marry me and were going to threaten me. Or something else, like he might ask me to run away with him and marry him. My curiosity got the best of me.

So I met with him. He told me he loved me and he would always love me. He cried. He was shaking like someone with a high fever. He laid his head down on my chest and then in my lap. We sat in the dark under a tree and I stroked his hair. I kept asking him, what was wrong, what was wrong. He grabbed me and clung to me and kissed me, and I clung to him, and he said, give yourself, and he was crying, sobbing, tears rolling down his face, and he said, give yourself to me. I love you. I need you. I'll never quit loving you, as God is my witness.

Well, you've met my daughter. That's how it happened. The next day, I found out what he had wanted to tell me was that he was marrying someone else. I could have killed my daughter or given her away, like other poor women do, but instead, I washed clothes to feed and raise her, and I never risked having more children. She doesn't appreciate it. Instead, she's mad at me for not giving her a father. That's how children are. They never understand their parents.

107

One Man

My son, he hasn't wanted to get married. He told me I never brought another man into his life when his father died, and he doesn't want to bring another woman into mine now. But I told him, I can't be around forever, especially now with this cancer. I'm in my eighties, and I can't be here for all of his life.

I had him late in life, almost forty, because I was going to be a nun, you see, but that didn't work out for me. Then I met a man and we married, and we lived fairly happily, except for his bad temper. And when my son was seven, his father died. I didn't want to risk any new man coming in and disciplining my boy, so I told him, you are the one man in my life now. I'm not going to date, I'm not going to remarry, and I'm certainly not going to allow someone else to discipline you. And my son appreciated it; he was grateful.

My son knew it was a lot of work for me, a woman alone in the United States with a little boy. No English to speak of. No real job skills, since you can't make a living off of playing the piano and embroidery. I suffered and struggled a lot, and several men I met offered to marry me and take me out of my misery, but I told them, there is only room for one man in my life, and that is my son. My son knew all this all along, and he appreciated it.

So I got him through high school and then into college, and he wanted to live at home during college, like our boys do back home. And I always wanted him to date or find a nice girl, but he told me, Mom, I'm happy with just the two of us; I don't need any other woman.

I don't like to think that I held my son back from having a family of his own, having his own children, and having a life when I'm gone. What is he going to do when he doesn't have me to cook and clean and keep house for him? What is he going to eat, and who is he going to talk to when he comes home from work in the evenings? I wish I could convince him to find some nice girl, someone I could get along with, and marry now. Then I could have a chance to be a grandma and to die in peace, knowing that he will be able to carry on.

But he says he is truly happy just the way things are. He said no one else will be able to cook like me, and no one will iron his clothes or take care of him like I do. He says there aren't any girls like me left anymore, that the modern girls are all work and demands. And now we've been alone together for forty years, five times as long as I lived with my husband. In some ways, we're like an old married couple. So now I'm just resigned to my fate and trying to stay alive as long as possible so I can keep taking care of my son, since he won't have anyone but me.

Onion Stalk

P lease tell the doctors, I was cleaning the field after the final harvest, and a
dried bit of onion stalk flew up and scratched me in the eye. I didn't think
much of it; I mean, it hurt, but we get scratched and bruised quite a bit in
the hurry of the harvest cleanup work. We get paid by the hour for that work, so
they really watch how fast we work. I have to work fastest of all, since I'm seventy-
three and some of the farms think I'm too old to work. Without a family of my
own, my only pension is my health.

So my eye was red and it hurt and it didn't get better, and I got an appointment at the Farmworkers Clinic. They gave me some creams and drops, but it
didn't get better. So they sent me to an eye doctor. He gave me two different treatments, and it didn't get better. It got white and dead-looking. Now the eye is very
bad, and I can't see out of it at all. I'd like to have it saved, but the doctors here
are saying I should have come before.

Tell the doctors, I did all the things I just said; I came as fast as I could. As
soon as that eye doctor said, look, I can't do anything more for you; you need to
see another specialist, you need to go to Seattle, well, I made the appointment as
soon as they let me, as soon as they gave me the referral. You see, we're not allowed
to just make an appointment. We have to get a letter in writing, or you won't see
us here. So as soon as I got the letter, I made the appointment. It really took five
months from the onion scratch to do all that.

Tell the doctors, I know I might lose the whole eyeball. They already told me
that. But tell them, also, from me, please, and I mean this from the heart: I believe in God and put my faith in Him. I know God has made them doctors, tell
them, and God has put the care of my eyeball into their hands, and I trust their
hands. So if they could find any way to save my eyeball and not take it out, I
would surely be grateful, but if it's not God's will for me to keep my eyeball, I
won't hold it against them. I believe God would not have put them into a position of power and allowed them to get all that schooling and work at such a big
hospital in such an important position if God didn't trust them. So please tell
them, I put myself in their hands—and God's. I won't feel resentful either way,
tell them.

The only thing is, since I am an older worker, and I don't have family, if there
was any way to save the eyeball, even if they couldn't make the vision very good
out of it, well, it might be hard to get work with one eyeball, that's all. But it's up
to them, tell them. Please tell the doctors that from me, and I'll be very grateful.
Either way, tell them, I'll be grateful.

Opening

T hank you for listening to all this, especially while I'm in labor. I know it's hard to hear about these things, these marital things. I know it's hard to believe that someone who was so cruel could also be missed, but I hope you understand. I don't miss him, who he is now. I miss the man he used to be. You met him; you remember him. I keep thinking about how he was. I can't take him out of my mind. He was so kind and so attentive, before.

We had five good years before he changed, and I can't get them out of my mind. I can't understand why that all disappeared, like it wasn't real. I know it was real; I lived it. How could a man not want what we had? How could a man not want to live in harmony with his wife and move forward with her? How could a man want his own wife to have to live in a shelter and be completely unprotected in this world? And carrying his baby, his own flesh and blood!

The doctor said I'm closing instead of opening. I think that talking about all this has made the baby move back up. I'm afraid I've scared the baby with all this, like the baby thinks it's not a safe place to come out into. Could you talk to the baby for me? He might listen better to you, since he knows I'm so upset. If you don't mind, you could just tell the baby this from me. It doesn't matter whether you say it in Spanish or English, because babies understand everything.

These things we discussed, they are not your fault and not your problem. You will have a home wherever you are, because your mother is your home, even after you are born. These problems we have talked about, they are your mother's problems, not yours. No one is going to hit you or insult you, because your mother will not allow that. It is safe for you to come out now. We are all here to welcome you. There is plenty of room in this world for you. That is why you were made. We have room for you and space for you, and you will have everything you need. Don't worry about anything. Just come on out and have no fear.

Thank you, I feel better now. We should have waited to talk about all this when the baby couldn't hear us, but something about the pain of labor brought it all to my mind. I'm glad I could unburden, and I hope the baby will forgive me for thinking of myself during this time.

I'm going to relax now, and think about opening up and letting the baby out. I think, I hope, that I'll be able to open up soon and let the baby out. I'm going to try my very best.

And baby, listen to me; this is your mother talking, I am opening up now to let you out, and I am going to protect you and love you, and if God grants us this wish, your father will become the man he was before, the man he was intended to be, and you will know your father.

Patron Saint

Did you ever want something so desperately that you just offered all kinds of things up to God if He would just please, please, let you have it? Well, I know a lot of people who did that and then they don't follow through, and I worry about how God will look at that later. So when my son was dying during childbirth, I was circumspect in my prayers, promising only what I could fulfill. And I have fulfilled my obligations and promises and commitments.

My son was named after his Patron Saint. He wears a necklace, which he has never taken off, with his Patron Saint's image on it. Each year, on his Patron Saint's day, I dress him up in traditional Indian clothes from my village, and I take him to Mass. Now that he is old enough to help, he helps to light the candles in front of his Patron Saint. I promised God I would do this with him every year until his seventh birthday, and now he is five. In two more years, he will decide for himself whether he wishes to continue. I hope he does. I think God will like it.

My son is very religious. He loves God his Father. He likes to pray, and he likes me to read the Bible to him. We have some children's Bible books, and he likes the stories of Daniel and the Lion and the burning bush and lots of others. He always asks us to read these stories to him. He doesn't care for Clifford, that big red dog, or those kinds of books as much.

Every night at bedtime, my son prays to God his Father. At first, I used to help him kneel down at his little bedside, and I would hold his hands together and help him pray in a baby way. Now, he does it himself, and I just kneel by his side. He prays for his relatives; he prays for his schoolteacher and little friends from school; he prays for anyone we know who is ill or unhappy; he prays for relatives who live far away; he prays for his Patron Saint and asks God the Father to keep him and protect him all the days of his life and to make me a good boy, he says.

Think if I had promised something like when he turns five, I'll send him to Rome. I know ladies who have done that, and then they don't have the money. See, Rome isn't a place you can get to by foot. You can't just grab a sack of rice and a pot to boil it in and start walking. You won't get there. How is God going to feel later when you can't get to Rome? This one lady, she was telling me, God is great. God knows our suffering, and He knows we can't get to Rome; He will understand. But I'm thinking, God does indeed know everything. He knows you were just asking for a favor, and at that very moment, He already knew you wouldn't fulfill it, see; He knows the future. So what use is an empty promise, which by its very nature God knows is empty at the very moment you breathe it out into the air? I honor God too much to lie to Him.

Picture

I think the best thing for a young man about living in the United States is being able to send money home to Mom. I mean, we all know how much our mothers have done for us, but few of us have the opportunity to really give anything back. Most of us just get enough money to scrape by. We continue to live under our mother's roof, eat her food, have her cooking and cleaning for us, and we just can't get anything together to do something really special for her. The local economy isn't set up for us to bring anything home but grocery money.

But me, since I live in the United States, I get to do really nice things for my mother all the time. I call her every Sunday and talk for twenty minutes. She really loves that. She tells me all the family gossip. She doesn't have a phone at home, so she has an appointment at the neighborhood phone center and gets my call there. It's become her Sunday outing. My brothers told me she dresses up for it, like church. And every month, I send her a remittance, usually at least a hundred dollars, sometimes a hundred and fifty if I get good tips.

This year, since I took a second job, I saved up five hundred extra dollars. I made arrangements to send the money to my brother-in-law who lives in the city. And he bought her just what I asked him to: a big huge color television for Mom to watch her soap operas on. It's cheaper than sending one from here. She's always had a black-and-white one, and it is just tiny. She has to sit right up next to it, and she can hardly see the picture.

I didn't want Mom to know about the television. I wanted it to be a big surprise. I called her the Sunday before Christmas, and I said, now Mom, things have been a little tight around here, so I hope you aren't too disappointed that all I sent you was an extra thirty-five dollars for you to make the Christmas tamales, just enough money for the holiday feast, I told her. She told me it was no problem at all. She had no idea she was about to get the biggest gift of her life!

On Christmas Eve at midnight—that is when we eat the main holiday meal— my brother-in-law asked my mother to sit down in the living room for a minute; he wanted to show her something he had in his car. And he and my brother carried in my color television. She was so surprised! She started laughing and crying and calling out my name. She knew I was the only one who could afford it. And she ran to her room and grabbed a picture of me I had sent her, and she taped it to the television set. Now, whenever anyone watches television, they have to look at my picture, because Mom won't let them take it off. Drives my brother crazy, but hey, he's not the one stuck in the United States working two jobs. I think it's pretty funny, myself.

Plugged

I hate to ask you for this kind of help—I know you can't do anything outside the hospital—but I don't know where to turn. I had a meeting at my son's school yesterday, and they had an interpreter, but he didn't do what you do. He just said some of what they said to me, like a summary. Then whenever I would try to talk, he would frown at me and interrupt me and say, you'd better just do what they're telling you, or you'll be in big trouble. This is serious.

I didn't have the words to tell them, so I was just stuck. The school principal, she demanded to know why my son had missed his medical appointment. She told me I have to take my son to the hospital, or they could get me in trouble for medical negligence.

They all think my son is deaf in one ear, or maybe both—I can't understand what they think—but they only think that because he's in third grade and he can hardly read or write at all. But they don't understand; he can hear fine. Just fine. I talk to him in a regular voice. He can answer back. I call him on the phone even, and he hears fine and answers just fine. Sometimes a stranger, like a teacher, will ask him a question and he won't answer, but that's because he's shy. Also, I have a sister who could never learn to read or write. She went to school for years, but nothing would stick. She just couldn't pick it up.

When I did take my son to the hospital to check his hearing, the assistant who checks the hearing told me my son had a hearing problem, and his hearing was uneven. Then she said they want to do a procedure, like a surgery, to plug one ear. Yes, plug one ear, so the other ear, like a lazy ear, would have to hear better. But I was trying to find out, if they plug the good ear, and his other ear doesn't work, couldn't he become deaf? How can they plug it without breaking the eardrum? Can they remove the plug, or is it forever? Why should I let them plug my son's only good ear, if he only has one good ear? Won't it take away what little hearing they think he has? And how come he can hear me fine? That's what I don't understand.

So when the second appointment came up, the one to see the doctor to plug his ear, I just didn't go. I mean, he can hear me fine. And now the school principal is saying she is going to call Child Protective Services, and they could come take my child. They don't know how that feels to me. They could come take him and plug his ear and maybe make him deaf, and the school principal says there's nothing I can do about it except go to the hospital and do everything they say. But why do I have to let them plug his ear when I can tell he can hear me just fine? I don't understand what they want, and I know for a fact they don't understand what I want to say.

Pork

I had already heard about how pork can be bad for you, so I never gave my baby pork, even though she does eat a lot of solid foods now. I don't think that can be what she has, that pork parasite that lays eggs in your brain. I think it must be something else. But it's strange, because it comes and goes. At least it did come and go the one time it happened before.

She was staying with my mom in Mexico so I could work longer hours to save up money. I don't make much as a housekeeper in hotels; they say they can't pay much because the economy is bad and there aren't enough hotel guests. So I took a job at two different hotels to get some money together. Then they called me in the United States to tell me that she had gotten numb on the right side and her hands clawed up. She is almost two years old, and her speech was getting pretty good. She could say at least twenty words and she was learning to greet my mother's neighbors by name, and she was great at walking, too. Then all of a sudden, last Wednesday, she just changed. Her right leg got weak and buckled under her. Both her hands seemed to retract, and she held them like claws. She lost all her words except "What? What?" And she lost her playful spirit and her energy. I couldn't believe what I was hearing.

We gathered up some money amongst relatives and flew her back here right away. I'm going to have a hard time paying them back, but they said no rush. I got her to the doctor here in Seattle, and they started doing tests. She saw a neurologist, and he has ordered more tests. I don't even know what all they looked for, but everything they thought it was, it wasn't. It seems like they have no idea what it is yet. It's nothing they know of, nothing they guessed.

I had hoped it was a onetime thing. Then today, it happened again, and I saw it myself for the first time. They weren't exaggerating. Her right leg, she would take two steps, and it would buckle up under her. She would fall down and then not even try to get up. She would sit there helpless, like she had lost her desire to try. Like she knows she can't walk anymore. As far as speech goes, she never got that back. She's lost all her words and her pronunciation.

I don't know what she has, but is there any chance they can finish the studies and let us know by the end of this month? President Bush has taken away our medical coupons, and we can't get any more health care after September. If I can just find out what kind of pills she needs to take, I can work long hours and pay for her medicines that way, without seeing a doctor. The doctor said it can take a long time to figure out what she has. Is there any way they could speed it up and figure out what she has by the end of this month? If not, then no hard feelings.

114

Praying

My wife and I moved here because I am a youth pastor for an Evangelical church in Mexico. They sent me to Pasco to work with youth on a five-year visa. I am in a poor neighborhood, just like our neighborhood at home, and have been successful in bringing a lot of young people back to God. My success has a lot to do with my wife. She is just a natural mother hen and caretaker for all these young people. She is a wonderful person.

My wife is 29 now, and I am 31. We have been married for eleven years. Unlike Catholics, we don't believe it's a sin to avoid having children while you finish school or do His work. We didn't use anything that could harm our fertility, though. I took care of her. That was up until four years ago, and then we started trying to have a family of our own.

We have gone through testing, and it seems like my wife is fine. You have children? So you may know about taking your temperature, watching your flow, checking all kinds of different things to see if your cycles are working correctly. They also did the test where they check my sperm count, and it was very low, but they don't know why.

My wife, she is taking this a lot harder than me. She is a good Christian, and like me, she is resigned to God's will. But you are a mother, so you can imagine how hard that would be to want to hold your own baby in your arms and then— nothing. She cooks and bakes for carloads of teenagers; sometimes children as young as ten want to participate in the youth ministries programs. We don't turn anyone away; we just open our hearts and homes. She acts as mother for quite a few of them, helping in the homework club and even the local Girl Scouts troop. You should see her around Christmas, when we have plays and concerts and caroling in town. She is so busy! This has been her life for eleven years, in different communities, always at my side.

Sometimes I tell her, honey, maybe you don't have time for a child of our own. Maybe it's God's way. But she says she reminds God every night at bedtime that while she is keeping busy doing His work, she can definitely make time if He, in His infinite wisdom, chooses to grant her a baby of her own. And she promises Him not to neglect His work if He does her this favor. She feels ready and open to love our own baby and keep loving the other children as well.

Today, they are going to do an ultrasound of my testicles and see if the vas deferens might be blocked. And if it's not, then we plan to end all this fertility treatment and just pray about it together, and let God know we are ready for a child of our own if He feels that we deserve it. I hope we do. I feel sure that my wife deserves to be a mother; she is so wonderful.

Professional

T hank you for calling me. No, I didn't mean to miss my Pap smear. Yes, I knew when it was scheduled. What happened was this. I had this male interpreter, this guy, you know? I know I was supposed to follow up on my abnormal Pap smear, but there I was with a man in the room. What could I do? It was too embarrassing. It's not like he is a doctor or anything; I mean, he's only an interpreter. So I told the doctor it was that time of month and couldn't have my Pap smear done.

So when we were setting the appointment for next time, I told him, look, no offense, but I would rather have my regular interpreter; she is a woman just like me. And he said, no, if I set the appointment, I get the appointment. Then he started talking a bunch of English with the staff, and he was looking at his calendar. I couldn't really say anything to staff.

So I gathered my courage, and I said, Sir, I appreciate your work and all that, but without wanting to offend you in any way, I really would prefer to have a female interpreter for my next appointment, and I can give you the name of my regular interpreter, if you want to tell the staff to schedule with her. And he turned to me and said, that won't be necessary. Then he told them (I know because I can understand some of what he says, but I can't really say anything back in English), she wants me. He said to the staff that I wanted him for the next appointment.

I was so embarrassed. I didn't know what to say or do. I was shaking and nervous. So I said, Sir, I want to be honest. I am a woman, and you are a man, and I am embarrassed to have you in the room for my Pap smear. This male interpreter, he just turned to me and said, Madame, I am a professional. I am not embarrassed, so you shouldn't be, either.

Well, I didn't dare say anything more. I just took the appointment he wrote down with me, and then I didn't go to it. That's how I missed my appointment. And what I was thinking, but didn't dare say, was, of course you're not embarrassed; you aren't lying on the table with your private parts exposed to someone who isn't even a doctor. Why would you be embarrassed? I'm the one who's exposed and embarrassed. You're just standing there looking.

I don't know why he said he was professional. A professional interpreter would have said what I said word for word, wouldn't he? In any case, I need to have a Pap smear as soon as possible, since my last one was abnormal, and if it turns out I have cancer, then may God forgive him. I don't know what you all are paid, but it can't be enough for the way he treated me, for him to fight for one hour like he did. I mean, doesn't he have any male patients he can work for?

Public Charge

I appreciate your offer to have me enroll in this program where you get all this pregnancy help and food and things, I really do appreciate it. It sounds nice to have a nurse and a social worker and a nutritionist and all that. But the thing is, my husband won't let me sign up for anything, because he said we are not allowed to become a public charge, or we can never become citizens. So we don't accept anything that might seem like welfare. We don't dare.

My husband has been working here for many years, and he now has his permanent residence. I am on a wait list to get permanent residence, but since we are Mexicans, our wait list is about twelve years. He has been taking the citizenship classes and hopes to take the test later this year. If he passes, then I wouldn't have to wait all those years to get my papers; I could get them right away. Citizens don't have to wait to bring their wives into the country.

But in the citizenship class, they told him that the United States only wants hard workers, independent people, you see. So that is why we don't get food stamps or medical coupons, even though we qualify for them, since my husband earns so little and I can only work part-time because of the children. I understand that you're saying none of this counts as welfare, but we just can't take the risk. Citizenship is just too important to us. It means everything.

We are hoping he can get his citizenship papers soon, because citizens earn more money and just have a better life in so many ways. For one thing, they can never be deported, and that is a huge change. Nowadays, even permanent residents are being deported right and left, from all kinds of countries. There is a big roundup going on as we speak.

But citizens, see, can never be forced out of the country, no matter who is president. We could live here as long as we want without fear or worry. All we have to do is last a few more years, working as hard as we can and paying our lawyer for the immigration papers, and then once my husband becomes a citizen, everything will be so much easier for us. Right now, things are hard because he can only work one job with the citizenship classes, and then we have this unexpected pregnancy, and I had to cut my hours. But we'll make it. We'll be okay.

So that's why I don't feel like I can take part in this program. I'll be fine with the food we have at home. Don't worry, I'll take good care of this baby, and I'll eat as much as I can this whole pregnancy. Thanks for the offer, I do appreciate it, but I just don't want to get kicked out of the country or stop my husband from becoming a citizen. I don't want to be a public charge.

Pulling Teeth

This doctor, I mean, was she deaf or what? I had to grit my teeth not to laugh out loud at her. I understand enough English to know it wasn't your fault she didn't understand. You told her over and over what I said, which is that I have never been to a doctor in my life. But she wouldn't stop asking. I can't wait to tell my wife about this; she'll never believe it.

We need to do a health screening before we pull teeth, she told me. When was your last doctor's visit? I haven't been to a doctor. Okay. When did you last go? I've never been to a doctor. Well, who is your doctor, then? I don't have one; I've never been to a doctor in my life. Okay, we have this questionnaire we have to fill out, to screen you for pulling the tooth.

Do you have asthma? No, I've never been to a doctor. Do you have diabetes? No, I've never been to a doctor. Do you have a heart murmur? No, I've never been to a doctor. Have you ever had a heart attack? No, I've never been to a doctor. Do you have seizures, like epilepsy? No, Mrs. Doctor, I've never been to a doctor. Do you have any digestive tract problems, like ulcers, chronic diarrhea, gallstones? No, I've never been to a doctor.

That's when I couldn't hold it; and I let out a little giggle. Then the doctor, she says, kind of strict, I have to ask you all these questions before we can pull the tooth. We have to know your health is fine so we don't pull your tooth and make you sicker. What if you have, say, AIDS, and we pull your tooth and you get an infection and you can't fight it?

God forbid! I tell her, I am only with my wife. Why are you talking to me about AIDS? I just want to get a tooth pulled; it's hurting so bad. Can't you just please pull it? I promise my health is good. I'm not lying to you. I've never been to the doctor. Nothing is wrong with my health. I'm not hiding anything, I assure you. I don't have any what you call health conditions. I'm not ill. Nothing bad will happen if you just please pull the tooth. I've had other teeth pulled, and I never got sick. I've never been ill in my life, I promise you. Can't you just cross off all the lines on that paper and go ahead and pull my tooth?

I'm sorry, the doctor tells me, I have to go down the list one by one and cross them off as you tell me. It's the rule. Have you ever had any sexually transmitted diseases, like HIV/AIDS? Do you have hemophilia? Arthritis? Liver problems, such as hepatitis? Tuberculosis? Have you ever had a stroke? Do you suffer from migraines? Take medication? Is your vision impaired?

Look, I finally told her, if you are looking for a reason to not pull my tooth, just tell me, and I'll go somewhere else. All I want is for you to pull this tooth. I'll sign anything. Please.

Quiet

Quiet! Quiet down right now, and sit down! Do you want the lady over there to spank you? Do you? Do you want her to come over here and spank you? Yes, that lady. She's getting mad at you! Children have to behave at the hospital, or they get punished. Do you hear me?

What are you doing? Shut that drawer. Those are medical supplies! Do you want to ruin everything? Don't you want the doctor to be able to help sick people? You can't play with the equipment. It's not a toy. I said shut that drawer!

What are you doing now? Leave that light alone. That's for the doctor to look at where babies come from. You don't want to play with that. Now get over here. Come. Come sit down. You sit here. Now. Sit still. Just be quiet, and the doctor will be here in a minute.

No, don't get down. What are you doing? You get back up here! I told you to quiet down and sit here. Do you want the doctor to poke you with a long needle when he comes in? Is that what you want? That's what the doctors do to especially disobedient children. The doctors keep extra-long needles, this long, see, to poke the bad children with. That way, the bad children will know to quiet down next time they come, because they won't want to get poked again. Do you want to get poked? I said sit down!

Okay, you can stand up, but don't stand by that door. If the nurse comes in, you will get knocked down. Then you'll bump your head and it will hurt and you'll get a bad, bad headache. I said get away from that door! Do you want the lady to get mad at you? She's getting mad at you! Get away from that door!

Get out of my purse. I already told you, I don't have any candy. Zip my purse up right now. Mami's wallet could drop out of it, and then we wouldn't have any money for the bus and we could never, ever get home and we wouldn't have money for food and when you got hungry, you wouldn't get anything to eat and I couldn't call anyone because I wouldn't have any money. No, your Papi wouldn't come save us, because he doesn't even know we're here. You don't know what would happen, so just shut my purse and quiet down.

Don't open that cupboard. That's where they keep the mean little dwarf that could come out and bite you. When you open the door, he gets surprised, and when he's surprised, he bites. I said, don't open the door! Of course you couldn't see him; he's invisible, silly. You're lucky he didn't bite you. Now come over and sit in my lap before the interpreter spanks you. She's smiling at you, but that doesn't mean anything. Get over here now and quiet down. I mean it.

Ranch

My mom warned me not to marry a city girl, but of course, love is blind. With all the people coming from all over the world to work in the United States, I guess I'm lucky I even found a Mexican girl, even if she is from Mexico City. I mean, I could have ended up with a Chinese lady or even someone from this country. Then where would we live? The problem is, now we are married and have this baby, we need to go home, but where is home for us now?

That's easy for me to answer. I want to go back to my ranch. I just know if she tries it out, she will love it. But she says she already knows, without even seeing it, that she won't like it! She says she knows I'll be out working on the ranch all day, and she'll be stuck in the house with my mom, cooking over a woodstove and washing clothes in the river. Well, we're not that bad off! We have well water and electricity.

My wife, she's never been anywhere where there was lots and lots of room. Where you hear crickets and sometimes frogs at night, and see fireflies and a huge swath of stars across an open sky. No traffic, no neighbors to look at. Just loved ones. You can sit on your porch for hours. Who needs television when you can just enjoy nature?

She talks about wanting to go to plays, the theatre, dance, and culture. With all due respect for the painters, who needs a painting of a sunset when I can see the sunset off my own porch? Who needs to see some beautiful lady dancing around half naked when I have my beautiful wife here to look at? Who needs to go to the zoo when you can take care of animals all day, your own animals that feed and clothe you and your family?

I think most of the things people do in the city are just to make up for not having the wholesome and healthy country living that human beings need by nature. Clean air, clean water, and food fresh from the farm. Butchering and eating an animal that you corn fed, that you raised from birth, is a lot different than buying some chunk of beef wrapped in plastic at the corner store, believe me! It's not a secondhand life on the ranch.

I'm sure the city has a lot of excitement, but what about peace and tranquility? What about relaxing instead of rushing around? What about children who can run around and just be kids all day long, never worrying about being kidnapped or hit by a car? My ranch is like a dream life, and I just know when my wife visits, she will agree to stay. She just doesn't know any better. A city is a nice place to visit, but it's no place to raise a family. She'll find that out if she just agrees to come to my ranch and give it a try. Nothing is better than the ranch.

120

Rancor

I'm a rancorous person. You know what I mean, vengeful and unforgiving. That's why I don't let my wife talk to her daughters even after all these years. They nearly drove us apart. They did everything they could to take her away from me. But who would take care of her like I do? No one. They all work; they don't have time for her. We're retired; we have time.

I am the one who takes her to the doctor. I carefully write down everything about her heart medicine, her insulin, her eye problems. Guess who draws up her insulin? I do! Guess who writes down her blood sugar? I do! I cook for her; I clean for her; I do everything for her.

Now her daughters all of a sudden find out she's ill, and they all of a sudden want to befriend her. I guess they feel guilty, but it's too late. They should have thought about that when they were teenagers, making up lies about me and trying to get her to choose between them and me. She chose me, all right, and the daughters moved out and lived their own lives.

There's no reason to forgive them. Besides, I've never forgiven anyone in my life. I'm not like that. I hold a grudge. I can remember every bad thing anyone ever did to me, and I can get myself all worked up about it just talking to you about it, years later. Yes, I am rancorous. I hold a grudge, all right. I tell you, as God is my witness, that I can get myself so worked up, just talking about this with you, that I would be ready to kill someone just for stepping in my path. They say I was born that way. At least, that's what my mom says; I never knew my father.

My wife, she's more kindhearted. She says, let bygones be bygones. We're not getting any younger. The past is gone. I tell her, no, I don't care if it was fifty minutes or fifty years ago; what's done is done and can't be undone. They made you choose, and you chose. That's that. She argues about it, in her meek way. She says her kids are her kids, and you can't change that; she says I don't understand, since I don't have any kids. She's wrong. I do understand, but that thing with her kids, it's all over. She'll never talk to them again, no matter how sick she gets.

I told her, if they come around trying to take you away from me, I'll kill them. I swear, I'll kill them and their husbands. And I'll leave you and never come back. You made your choice, I told her, now you stick with it. They said me or them, remember, and you said me. I won't stop you. But you change your mind, you'll never see me again. And they won't be able to take care of you like I can. Some of the hospital staff, they try to tell me, your wife is ill; she wants to see her children. You have to let her. But no, I don't. I'm a rancorous person. I wasn't raised to forgive, and I'm not going to start now. Even if I wanted to, I wouldn't know how.

Rape

I supervised workers in a factory back home, so I knew a lot of women. One of my employees, her husband had died, and she used to have her thirteen-year-old take care of the younger four children. Her daughter started to act strange, and scared, and finally my friend was able to discover that she had been raped repeatedly by a neighbor. It was an old man, and he had told the girl that he would kill her mother if she ever told anyone. So she never mentioned anything until she found out she was pregnant, and that was when she finally told her mother.

The man fled the area once people knew about him. My friend, the mother, felt so bad, but as a widow, she couldn't both stay home and feed her children at the same time. She really had no choice. It is horrible to feel that you can't both feed and protect your children. But if she hadn't worked, they could have literally starved to death. Besides, how could she know her neighbor would turn out to be a rapist? She thought her children were safe while she worked.

The most amazing thing was the girl. She was thirteen when all this happened to her. Her mother offered to help her do what people do in that situation: terminate the pregnancy. The girl chose not to do that. They talked about adoption, but the girl chose not to do that, either. This wasn't like a huge, philosophical discussion I'm talking about; these are humble people, people with very limited resources. They had a very hard choice to make, with no easy way out.

In the end, the girl chose to have the baby and keep the baby, and at the age of fourteen, she gave birth to a healthy child. She hadn't had the opportunity for school, so it didn't affect her studies. And I don't know how she found the strength to go through the childbirth at her tender age, but she did. Not by choice, but by force of circumstance, and accepting that force.

I saw the girl two years later. She was working in a small café, a modest, wayside restaurant. She helped with cleaning up, making the tortillas, that sort of thing. She did most of her work with her son on her hip and sometimes sat him down at her feet while she worked. And he was alive—something most people would think he didn't have a right to be—but there he was. A perfectly normal boy who could have been denied the gift of life. And she was the only one who could give him that gift, make something so miraculous out of such a horrible situation.

I respect that girl so much. I just can't forget her. Whenever I have to make a hard decision, I remind myself that there are harder choices in this life, and younger, weaker people with fewer resources are making good decisions all the time. They are truly heroic. And me, I just try to be better than I am, to deserve to be a part of humanity with them.

Remission

I swear to you I never even heard the word remission before. I don't even know what it means. All I know is these doctors did surgery on my wife's brain tumor last year, and they didn't say this remission word. They said the cancer was gone. Cured. They said they got everything, and it was out. Removed. I never heard about remission. And I take issue with that. I take issue with the doctors. These doctors here, they said it was gone. So I don't know why now, all of a sudden, they say they meant remission all along, because that's not what they said.

They told me it was gone, that there was no more cancer, do you understand? They said my wife was well, and she was. She went home, and except for the scars on her head, she was as good as new. They said she was cured. Then her head started to hurt again. Not all at once, but little by little. And it just got worse and worse until she couldn't take it. It got so unbearable that she told me, take me to the hospital and have them give me a shot so I can die, because death is better than this pain! She was screaming in agony.

I had to take her to the emergency room. They gave her a shot of the highest dose of the strongest painkiller they have, they told me. And it took three shots and five hours before her pain was under control, because it hurt that bad. That's when they found out the cancer had come back. They said the remission was over. And we said, what remission? What is that?

We had never heard about remission, only about cure, you understand? And her pain has been unbearable. Now they say it's too dangerous to operate, but I don't care. It can't be worse than this. Take away her pain, tell them, and I don't care if she can't do anything but lie around in bed or in a chair night and day without moving—just lie around like a baby or a helpless child—and I will lift her in and out of bed and do everything myself. Cleaning, cooking, bathing her, everything. I don't care if she can't even move her hand or foot or even feed herself. I can feed her and move her and do everything, as long as I have her and she isn't in pain.

The thing that hurts me more than anything is for her to be in pain. For her to cry and sob and cry and sob and tell me, Honey, I just can't take this. It's too much for me. I can't take it. That tears me up inside. It just tears me up, and if they could just—please tell them from me—just take her pain away, I don't care if she is completely disabled. See, the doctors told me she was cured, and now, all of a sudden, they say it's inoperable, but I want them to operate again. Tell them, I don't care if they take half her brain out. Just fix her. Then I'll take care of her like I have all these years. But no remission this time; just do a good job and cure it for good. Okay?

123

Ride

See, I wasn't going to take her husband from her. Honestly, I was just giving him a ride to the fields every day, because I was the one with the car, and I went around picking people up who worked with me, no big deal, nothing personal, you see. And sure, he liked me and I liked him, friendly like, nothing romantic, you understand. Just run-of-the-mill, friends-at-work kind of thing. Then his wife had to get all bent out of shape about nothing. For no reason at all.

All I did was call him a couple times if I was going to be late or early or if something came up. It wasn't like I was trying to make a point or claim territory or anything. But she would be rude to me on the phone, like, oh, is that you again? Hmm. Well, let me see if he's busy. I think I told you he had some family things to do, and I wasn't sure when he could call you back. Do you have a problem? Do you want to leave a message? This is his wife, she would always say, like I didn't already know who she was. I mean, I knew who she was.

And anyway, I mean, the guy was five years younger than me; he had his family. What would I need a guy like that for? I swear, I was just giving him a ride. I mean, what was he supposed to do? Walk to the fields? It was helping his wife, too, to have me giving him a ride. I mean, I drove him to work every day, and his wife got to stay home. So what was the problem?

Well, he ended up confiding in me that his wife was jealous of me! She had accused him of wanting to be with me, to cheat on her. That was ridiculous! I had never lifted a single finger to draw him my way. So what if we talked in the car and joked around? It wasn't like a love affair! I knew he was a young, married man. What would I want with a guy like that?

But then his wife, she called and accused me! She accused me of trying to break up their marriage. She said she knew through the others that I was flirting with him and offering myself, and she said a lot of worse things before she was done. I was very offended and I got mad, and I ended up telling her, you think I've been trying to take him from you? Well, I haven't been trying. But guess what? Since you brought it up, I will try now! And you'll see the difference! But remember, you asked for this. You brought it on. So don't come crying to me later.

See, all I was doing was giving him a ride. Nothing more, nothing less. I had a car, and he needed to get to the fields. I think I know enough about right from wrong to know what I did and what I didn't do. And if his wife hadn't accused me of anything, I never would have taken him from her, but I was getting in trouble for it, so I figured I might as well do it. But honestly, until she called me, all I was doing was giving him a ride. That's all. And now he lives with me.

Royal Jelly

t's just that we've always been so healthy, my husband and I. Unusually so. People comment on it; they think it's strange and lucky. But I think it is probably this special vitamin thing we buy in Nuevo Laredo. I still have my people there, so they can send it to us fresh. It's called royal jelly and it's made with honey. My whole family's been taking it for years, and it really preserves your health. But since I got diabetes, my doctor told me I had to stop taking it since it has so much sugar, and now I got this cancer. He told me he would give me a different kind of vitamin that was just as good and wouldn't hurt me, but as it turned out, the doctor's vitamins are not the same as my royal jelly. They didn't protect me and I got cancer.

My husband, he didn't go to the doctor for twenty years. He never felt the need, he told me. He thinks doctors are mostly just for women anyway, you know—female problems and childbirth and things. But after I found out I had cancer, I told him, I said, now honey, look how quickly things can change with your health. One day I was fine, the next day I had diabetes, and now I have cancer. Why don't you just give me peace of mind and go to the doctor?

So he did, and the doctor brought me into the room and said, Lady, what the heck are you doing to your husband? I don't understand! He weighs the exact same amount he weighed when I last saw him twenty years ago. The exact same number of pounds; it's like a miracle. His blood pressure is exactly the same. He hasn't changed a bit, and absolutely nothing is wrong with him! What are you feeding him! And I told him, I said, Doctor, I think it must be the royal jelly I get from my people in Nuevo Laredo. We all took it for years, and I had to stop, and now I've gotten sick, but my husband stays the same—pure health. I asked the doctor, could I take it with diabetes?

The doctor, he said he couldn't tell me what to do about my health, since I'm not his patient, but he told me to make sure my husband keeps doing everything exactly the same, since it sure is working for him. Then he shook my hand and told me I sure was a wonderful wife, and he recommended that my husband keep me around, ha ha! My husband said he plans on it, and he'll keep taking the royal jelly, too.

I understand the diabetes doctors; they are just trying to keep me from having high blood sugar. They told me it can cause blindness and even amputations, but I sure wish they would let me take some royal jelly, even twice a week. I think it would help with this cancer. Do you think if they gave me more insulin, I could take my royal jelly? Could you ask them?

Running

My son is a good boy. He is kind and courteous, and I know he loves me. He doesn't disrespect me. He takes care of me a lot. He is thirteen years old, just on the verge of manhood. But the other day, he ran away. We were discussing something at the house, and he just walked out the door, took off running, and disappeared down the street. I didn't know what to do!

I am not well, I cannot move very fast, and my youngest child was at home. There was no way I could chase him down. I was terrified! And our discussion was something stupid, not important at all, like homework or chores, just a routine thing, and then he panicked and darted off like a scared rabbit. I didn't know what to do! I left my child with the neighbor and borrowed a car and went to all his friends' houses, but no one had heard from him. Just at dark, thank God, I found him at the park at the corner. He was sitting on a bench all alone, just staring off into space like a condemned man with no future.

I made him get into the car. I was so mad and so relieved at the same time! I wanted to hug him and punch him and hug him again! Only God knows how much I love that boy. He means the world to me! So I asked him, Son, what in the world is going on here? What happened to you? Why did you run away? I just couldn't help it, he told me. I just felt so bad, I had to leave. I'm sorry, Mami.

But why would you leave if you feel bad, Son, I asked him. How is that going to help anything? If you need to talk, why don't you talk to your mother, the woman who loves you and understands you more than anyone else in the whole wide world and the only one who carried you inside of her and loves you more than her own life, Son? Why don't you talk to me?

So he told me, Mami, I feel bad. I feel angry and then I disobey you, and then I feel guilty and I feel sorry for you, because my dad's a drunk, and now he's in jail for drunk driving, and I hate him and I love him and I love you and I feel sorry for you, and why does my life feel so bad and wrong, and then I feel sorry for you, like your life is even more messed up than mine, so why can't I just be a good boy and mind you so you won't have the added pressure of having a bad boy to worry about? That's why I feel like running away. I hate myself, and I hate my life.

The saddest thing about hearing him say this was that all I have been doing for the last twenty years of my life is trying not to hurt anybody, trying to protect my kids and make sure they are okay, and they are not okay. Everything I did, all my sacrifices, have added up to nothing. So I just sat alongside my son, and we were in the car for a long time, sobbing.

Rush

I don't know what the doctor's so mad about. She acts like I'm wasting her time, but I'm the one who's been sitting here all day long. She comes in here yelling at me about why am I back today when I just had an appointment yesterday. Well, I'd tell her if she'd be quiet long enough and not rush me around like a cow being led to the slaughter.

I found out yesterday I have gestational diabetes, so I'm going to have diabetes for the rest of the pregnancy. Fine. I got the information on it; they gave me that little machine and the things to poke yourself with. I sat for an hour with a doctor or specialist or whatever, and they showed me how to draw up and inject the insulin into my thighs. Fine.

Last night, I gave myself my first dose and ate dinner. Then I got dizzy. I got shaky. I got a headache. I felt weak. The nurse had told me, call if you get those symptoms. So I did. I was told to! I tried to tell the nurse in English that my sugar after dinner was 220, and what my symptoms were. I don't know how much she got. She didn't give me an interpreter.

The nurse talked to the doctor, and then she called me back and left me three messages, and each message said the same thing, as far as I could understand the English. It looks like you have an adverse reaction to the insulin. DO NOT USE ANY MORE INSULIN! Do not inject yourself at all, and come straight to the clinic in the morning for the doctor to check you.

So I came in, and the same diabetes lady showed me the same thing over and over again, even though I already understood it the first time. How to inject myself. How to draw up the insulin. How to check my blood sugar. How to write it in the little notebook. Now she's saying it's okay for me to use insulin, when last night, it wasn't. Then they said, wait here until the doctor can see you. And I have waited all day. Really, I'm not exaggerating. I have been here six hours, since eight o'clock this morning. The lady at the desk said I can't get in until somebody no-shows because I didn't have an appointment! But they called me three times and told me to come in! That sure sounds like an appointment to me.

And now this doctor I've never even seen before comes in and yells at me about how could I have low blood sugar symptoms when I had a high blood sugar reading. How the heck would I know? I've only had diabetes since yesterday! Anyway, what's she so mad about? I'm the one who's sick and pregnant, waiting for six hours in the waiting room. Believe me, I'm in a lot bigger hurry to get through the rest of this pregnancy than she is! And you can tell her that from me when she comes back in the room. Actually, don't. I don't want her to get mad at me.

Sacred Heart

I was visited by the Virgin of the Sacred Heart, and no one can take that away from me. Some people believe; some people don't believe. It makes no difference to me. I have my knowledge. I have my proof. I wasn't delirious, like some people have hinted.

Okay, I had had surgery, and a lot of drugs. I readily admit it. I was close to death. I admit that, too. But that doesn't explain what happened to me in the dead of the night, when no one in the hospital was anywhere near me and I felt my life waning away, leaking out of me never to return. I felt a heavy pressure on my chest, like a devil was sitting on me and stopping me from breathing. I struggled to get in a breath, but I couldn't, and that is when I felt myself fading away, bleeding from the surgery and drifting off into oblivion.

Then, at the last possible moment, when no one else was there, light! The room was filled with a soft, glowing, warm, and pervading light. Not like the hospital lights that make you squint, but like, ah, I don't have words to describe it. Like candle glow, but warmer, softer, more peaceful, something that just makes you restful and you fall back into it like a soft, soft pillow.

The pressure on my chest lifted, and all of a sudden, I was breathing freely. I felt no more pain, no more suffering. I felt a presence in the room, and I saw, at the side of my hospital bed, just like I'm looking at you right now, I give you my word of honor, the Virgin of the Sacred Heart. She was beaming down on me with a look of infinite compassion.

She was the one glowing, glowing with that angelic, holy light. She wore a white, flowing robe, and on her chest, I could see the sacred heart, bleeding, and surrounded by thorns. She took my hand, and she said, do not be afraid. Do not succumb to worry. Are you not in God's hands? Will He not take care of you? You will survive. He knows your mother's heart. He will keep you safe to care for your children. Now sleep, and you will sleep all night, and when you awake, you will feel relieved of your pain and your suffering.

That is what the Virgin of the Sacred Heart said to me, and she took a beautiful pillow, and she put it under my left hip and laid me back upon it, and my pain was gone. And I slept. And I slept all night until the next day, and nothing they did could rouse me to this world until then. They were sure I would die! They prodded and poked me all night. But I survived!

Here is my proof: I have the pillow still, the beautiful pillow. And no one has ever seen it before, and none of the nurses or anyone knows where it came from, except me and God.

School Bus

I've been driving a school bus for fifteen years now, mostly on the same route. The parents and teachers seem to like me, since they send notes and ask for me to be the bus driver for the following school year. I go to a special education center with preschool kids who are disabled. They are always scared when they start, but I try to be extra kind and gentle with them, and after a while, they get excited and happy when they see me driving up in the bus.

Most of them can't talk at all, even when they are five; they are called nonverbal kids. But they will make noises like little animals, and I can see in their faces and gestures if they are happy or sad. I have learned some sign language to talk to them as well—just a few things like thanks and goodbye. I'd like to learn more words, like scared and curious, but I just pick it up from the kids, so my sign language is pretty basic. It's still good to be able to say a few things.

It's the most beautiful program, this special education. Sometimes I get to go into the viewing area with a one-way glass mirror, and I can't help admiring this program. The children have wonderful toys and activities and there are lots of nice young people, like teaching and nursing students, who play with them and cheer them on as they make their accomplishments.

A lot of the children use wheelchairs, and I carry them onto the bus and make sure they are safely fastened. One boy who wasn't in a wheelchair kept unbuckling himself, and then I had to pull the bus over. So an aide rode with him for a while and they told his mother, look, your kid is too much trouble. He yells and screams and bangs his head, and he won't stay seated. He isn't what you call appropriate for our program. They gave him a week to improve or leave.

I had this feeling he was just scared, and that's why he was trying to get off, so I talked to him. I looked right in his face and told him a lot of things about the program and how great it is and how nice everyone is. I went ahead and told him in Spanish, since I think disabled kids understand from your face and your tone of voice what you mean anyway. And he still screamed for a few days and rocked his head, but he didn't unbuckle himself, and they let him stay. Now he's doing fine. He's really improved a lot. I think this school is the best thing for him.

Starting this fall, the Seattle School District laid off my company and hired a nonunion shop to save money. They might hire me, for less pay, but they said they can't give me my same route. I'm going to miss those special kids. I hope the new guy will be patient, because that's important with disabled kids. Believe it or not, some of the school bus drivers don't like kids. I don't understand that. How can you not like kids? They're all so wonderful.

Scolding

Now listen up, Grandson. You were just born about two minutes ago, and I know this is all new to you. You wouldn't come out, so your mother had to have a Cesarean section to get you out; that's why Grandma is holding you. Your mother can't hold you; she is still getting stitched up from the surgery, so you will be in Grandma's arms for a while longer yet. Now listen up, Grandson, and listen good.

Your mother has already sacrificed a lot for you. She has brought you into this world, and you have to respect her. She is the number-one person in your life, and without her, you have nothing, not even a body to live in. Don't fall asleep when I'm talking to you! Grandson!

Listen. You have to be a good boy. A very good boy. I don't want to see any tantrums, or running around, or disobedience. You are here on this planet now, and you have to follow certain rules. Your mother knows all these rules, and she will instruct you. Listen to her, obey her in all things, and your life will be very good. Otherwise, no, Grandson. You don't want to go bad. Bad boys are a terrible burden on their mothers. You have to be a good boy at all times.

Look at me. I know the light is bright in here, but look at me, and listen. You must behave well at all times. Be a good boy and mind your mother. She deserves all your respect, and she always has your best interests in mind. Don't be looking at me like that; what are you frowning for? Are you glaring at Grandma? Don't glare at Grandma! Bad boy!

No, grandson, don't cry! I'm not mad at you. I promise. I'm only telling you things you need to know to get by in this world. Shhhh—shhhhh. Hush, don't cry, little one. Calm down, now. Calm down. You're taking this all wrong. Don't be so sensitive. I only scold you because I love you so much, and I want you to have a good life. You know we all love you!

Don't be scared, Grandson! Your mother is a kind person. She will take good care of you, and she will love you a lot. You know that; you lived inside of her. You know her heart. You have nothing to fear, Grandson. I know it's a lot of responsibility, but that's how it is. Children must respect their elders, or the whole thing falls apart; that's why I'm telling you this.

I'm glad you calmed down. These early lessons can be hard ones, but I wanted you to know. This lady here, she is your mother. She will be the center of your life for a long, long time, and I just wanted to introduce you. Now here, I'll bend you over her face so you can give her a son's kiss. That's a good boy. Now you've had your first scolding, you can go back to sleep and relax for a bit. As soon as your mother feels better, she'll put you to her breast.

Separation

My husband wanted to dominate me, but he couldn't. I wouldn't let him. He could not impose his will on me, and that made him mad. When I got pregnant, he started to worry all the time. In our village, we have this belief that what the mother does and thinks will change who the baby becomes, so he kept telling me, you must think this, you must think that, you must pray for a male child. Hold your mind to it, he would tell me. You can make it a boy.

No, I told him. I can't do that. All I can ask God is for the baby to be healthy and to be strong. That is enough for any parent to ask. We can ask no more; it is disrespectful to God. What if I insist on a boy and then the boy is unwell? Health is the primary consideration.

My husband didn't believe me; he kept telling me to not eat that, and to eat this, to make it be a boy. Sit like this, get up like that. Hold it in your mind, hold it in your mind that it will be a boy; don't let go of that. He would even wake me up to make me change sleeping positions.

When my daughter was born after three days of labor, I hemorrhaged. I fell to the floor and passed out and knew nothing until the next day. I woke up very weak. I didn't remember anything about the baby, except that it was born.

When I woke up, I saw that my husband was very sad, like a different man. I saw him crying by the bedside. I thought our baby had died or was some kind of monster.

What is it? I asked him. Is the baby all right?

Yes, yes, the baby is fine, he told me. Then I realized he must be crying about me.

Don't worry about me, I told him, I'm going to be fine. I lost a lot of blood, but the doctors are giving me a transfusion, and I'm going to be fine. Don't worry about me.

I'm not worried about you, he told me suddenly with cold, angry eyes. You made it a girl. You knew I wanted a boy first, but you made it a girl. I asked you to hold it in your mind that it was a boy, but you refused. You selfishly wanted a girl, and you made it a girl

He told me he was leaving me; he wanted a separation. You'll be sorry, he told me. You could have had a good life with me. But you threw it all away when you disrespected me. You just used me to get your daughter. You never really loved me.

I thought it was just the shock of the birth that he was so upset and angry, but it wasn't. We lived together for three more months, and then I had to leave him because he was beating me. I had to move out, and now I never see him, and he never sees us. That's what separation is. It's like dying. He's just gone.

Share

Yes, I knew he was married when I moved in with him, but his wife and kids were in Mexico. They couldn't join him, since he has legal permanent residence, not citizenship, and they are wait-listed for about a decade before they can come to the United States.

I've had boyfriends, but I've never fallen in love before. This man was different. So tender, so upright and good. He told me about the family and his commitment, but it made me love him more to know he was so responsible. He was so lonely, he even got an ulcer. These are life circumstances God puts in our path, and God alone knows why He does it.

After about a year, I moved in with him. I was so happy! I would get up at 5:00 a.m. and make him a strawberry-and-banana milk shake and serve him cornflakes and pack him a solid lunch. When he got home, I would have dinner ready, and he could eat a nice, hot meal before going to his second job. His ulcer got better, and he was happier. In the winter, I used to put his clothes in the dryer before he got dressed so he could get into warm clothes in the morning.

Then, in one of life's mysteries, his family visa came through, and he had to leave me and go to California to be with his real wife and kids. How I miss him! And that was right after our baby was born, our sweet little boy. And I worried about how I would be able to take care of a little baby all by myself, but I was able to find a nice lady to watch him while I work, and God helped me to find a job in a factory. So God has been compassionate toward me.

My friend's wife found out about me because I had to call him about some important papers that came to my address. It was from Immigration, so I called his sister and asked for him, and he was there, but so was his real wife, and she got on the phone and yelled at me and said quite a few things to me, but I didn't answer back, not one word, because who am I really to fight over something that doesn't belong to me? It's not my place to do so, and I'm a Christian.

He's made an agreement that he'll live with his wife and try to get along, and if he can't, once he's got her papers and the kids' papers in order, he will divorce her and come back to me. He said he's never been as happy as I have made him, and we never fought or argued; we always just felt like we were living in a beautiful dream. My mom always said, if you can't be pretty, at least try to be pleasant, and I did try to please him as much as I could!

My girlfriends ask me, aren't you sorry you got involved with a married man? But I can't regret anything, because of my beautiful baby. God in His mercy will decide our fate.

Shooting Blanks

It's been very rough, this infertility. But we're going to get it taken care of. It's just hard when the families get involved and start giving advice. You know, you get calls from the father-in-law, joking around and asking you why you're shooting blanks, what's wrong with your pistol, don't you load it right, and all that. That's hard to take. And time is passing. That's why we decided to seek infertility treatment. I've done what I can at home, and now we need help.

See, I've lived in this country for years and years. So I am not a prude about sex.

Not to brag or anything, but I've had sex for years. It took me a long time, though, to get used to the idea that it was okay. Where I was raised, we were taught that sex is a big huge sin, really bad and dirty and shameful, and married couples can do it, but mainly to have children. And that's how my wife was raised, too. And she hasn't gotten over it. She still feels bad about it.

My wife here, I just brought her up from Mexico a year ago. She was a virgin when we married, and everything she did, she did in shame, even though we were married in the church. I really think that's why she can't get pregnant. How could you get pregnant if you are so uptight and closed and hard all the time, like you are only doing it because it's your duty, but it fairly disgusts you? How could you get pregnant that way? She doesn't like to touch or be touched.

I've tried everything I can to get her to open up. I've been telling her for a year now, sex is normal. It's no big deal. It's a natural event. But her painful modesty keeps her closed up and tight, and I think the sperm can't get up there and get to work. I'm telling you the truth when I tell you I've tried everything, even renting movies to show what other people do, to show it's all normal. Nothing has worked. She said the films are disgusting, and she only feels worse after watching them. She just won't try anything new or different. She is closed to all of it.

So I gave up on the films, and I started just trying to do everything nice for her. No pressure, just lots of kissing and caressing and telling her how much I love her. All the things I see the men do on the Brazilian soap operas she likes to watch. Oh, my darling, and all that. I wake her up with a kiss, I hold her in my sleep, we walk around holding hands all day, I brush her hair at night, but I don't know. She still doesn't get pregnant.

I think it's a good idea to get this fertility screening, but I am pretty sure nothing is wrong with me. And I don't really think anything is wrong with her, either. I just wish I could figure out the best way to help her relax and have fun. I think if I can win her over, and have her really enjoy sex, she would open right up and get pregnant. Maybe this doctor will have suggestions.

Soap Opera

D o you watch soap operas? I do. I think the Mexican ones are the best, because they follow a nice plot, and in the end, the people you like end up happy, and the people you don't like are duly punished. I think it's a fun way to reward myself for taking such good care of all my children and the house. But my husband likes to tease me about it.

How can you still be in love with that man when you've seen how many times he's been unfaithful to you, my husband will ask me, talking about the main actor. Look, there he is kissing yet another woman! I'd like to see how long you would stay in love with me if I tried any of those tricks on you! You're so gullible with that man! Can't you see what he's up to?

Then he tries to convince me that no one really feels the emotion that the people in the soap operas do. He says it's like that fake wrestling, where they pretend to hit each other, but they really don't. In the soap operas, he tells me, it's all false emotion. But I don't see it that way. It's more like a really good novel. And in a really good novel, they say it reflects life. It rings true, and that's why people like to read the old classics even a hundred years later.

In the soap opera I'm watching, for example, a woman married without love, to gain financial security. Well, we all know that can happen. Then the man, who was a lot older, dies and leaves her a widow. But see, he kind of knew she didn't love him that much, so in his will, he sets it up so the estate is held by the wife only until each of the three daughters marry. Then each daughter in her turn gets a third of the estate, and the mother is left with nothing.

The mother, of course, never tells the daughters this. They are still minors when their father dies. So the whole soap opera, the girls are trying to date, trying to have boyfriends, eventually trying to get married, and the mother is actively trying to stop them every step of the way. Now, most mothers don't need their daughters to stay single for that reason, but isn't it pretty typical also that we try and stop our daughters from dating for one reason or another?

For example, my husband. He says the soap operas are all fake, yet when I teased our kindergartener and called the cute little white boy in her class "son-in-law" and joked about them getting together, didn't my husband get mad and say his daughter will never date? Didn't he joke that he would buy a pistol when she got older? And now, with this ultrasound, didn't I tell him he better buy a machine gun instead, and didn't he understand then, we're having another girl, and didn't his face light up with protective joy? See, it's not exactly like a soap opera, but they do draw from life. They remind us of ourselves. That's why I really enjoy my soap operas.

Son

Look at him! What a big boy he is! You little brute! You little roughhousing guy, you. Look at those muscles. By God, all you need is a moustache, little fellow, and you'd look just like your grandpa. Look at him kicking it up and grimacing like all get-out. Look at him! Who would have thought he would look just like this? Isn't it just so amazing?!

Ha ha! What a face. A face only a mother can love. Nah, I'm just kidding, son. You know Papi loves you; you know your old man thinks the whole, wide world of you, don't you, boy? Yes, you do! I can see it on your face! Don't try to fool the old man, son; you won't get far with that one, ha ha! You know you're a handsome devil, don't you, boy?

What a character! Just a few hours old, and so much personality! He's a handful, all right. Yes! You heard me! You're a handful, aren't you, little fellow? You gave your Mami a run for her money trying to get out, didn't you, little guy? You did quite a bit of kicking it up inside, too, now didn't you? Yes, you did. Yes, you did!

Where do you get all that energy from, son? You're going to be hard to keep up with; I can tell already. Here you are, fresh and new to this world, and you're just raring to go! What a strong little boy you are, yes, you are! Look at your little ears, look at your hands! You have long fingers—good, strong hands. You're a real little man, you are.

Look at him, honey. Have you ever seen anything like it? I can't believe it. What a guy! What a perfect little guy. Did you ever dream you were walking around calm as could be with this little man kicking it up inside of you? Did you ever think he would be like this? Look at him! Oops, he needs a diaper change!

No, give him back to me; I can change his diaper. I can do it. He's my little man; that's right, little man. You're Papi's boy, aren't you? You and me, we're going places, son. We're going to do everything together. You are one special little fellow. Now, don't get me wrong; you're going to respect your Mami. And you're going to mind her. And she's going to play with you, too. We both love you, but I have a feeling you're going to be Papi's special buddy.

There you are. Look at those tiny little buns. Look at those rosy thighs. Aren't you just the perfect one? Aren't you just the little man! Just a minute, now, son; don't kick yourself off the table. Give me a chance to get the new diaper on. There's a first time for everything, you know. Whoops. Whoa! Honey, honey, look! Look quick! Little Buddy Boy here is peeing on the ceiling! Bravo! Bravo, little man!

Sorry

My son was feeling sick for a long time before they diagnosed him. He was six months old when I noticed these changes. He started bruising very easily, and he lost weight. He became very weak, like he didn't have any energy, and he went from crawling and sitting to just being flaccid like a jellyfish. Over time, he lost all his muscle tone and was like a dying old man, just lying there staring with a glassy look.

I was going to the clinic in my town in eastern Washington, and I took him in, I don't know, five or six times at least. If you are a mother, you know what I'm talking about when I tell you I knew. I knew he was sick and he could die, but I couldn't make the doctor believe me—not by crying, not by scolding, not by threatening, not by pleading. Not even by bringing my husband in to the clinic to ask her to please, please help us. And our baby was growing weaker.

Finally, after two months, the doctor said that just to please us, she would draw blood and run some lab tests, and then we really needed to just relax and quit worrying so much. A lot of babies are tired sometimes, and ours looked just fine to her, she told us. So they drew blood, and the next day the nurse called us and said we had to go to the big hospital, in Seattle. But she didn't tell us anything about what they had found out or why we had to go.

We drove for four and a half hours, and when we arrived, we found out our appointment was in oncology. That means cancer. The doctor came in and started talking to us about leukemia, which is what our son had, but he didn't know our own doctor had never told us anything. He was surprised that we were surprised, and he ended up calling her about it.

We stayed in the hospital for a few weeks and then moved to a Seattle apartment to stay for the first year of treatment, since we have to be at the hospital almost every day. During that first week in the hospital, guess who called me? The doctor from our clinic! She called and told me she was sorry she hadn't believed me. She even cried.

She cried on the phone and begged our pardon. And saying sorry doesn't make it right—I don't know how much harm was done to our son by waiting those months—but maybe it means that she won't do the same thing to another family, and at least that is a comfort. Some of our friends told us the doctor probably only apologized so we won't sue, since lots of parents sue the doctors here, but we're all human, and we're all in God's hands. We just hope that when she says she's sorry, she really means it from her heart. If God has opened her eyes, if she has become a more careful doctor because of our son, if she's really and truly sorry, that's better than nothing.

Spooked

When did I become disoriented and lose control the first time? I don't like to talk about this, but you seem like a sincere person. Listen, I was spooked, you know? It was my grandchildren's father's sister-in-law, his brother's second wife, who did it. Thank God—God is great—and they have since been deported. But at that time, they were staying with us, and I was home alone with them, and it was up to me to serve them food and take care of them while my daughter was at work.

I was cooking in the kitchen, preparing everything and making things nice, getting the plates ready, and I turned around. My grandchildren's father's sister-in-law was looking at me like this—a burning stare. I felt like she was going to burn a hole right through me—may God protect me from harm. My heart is beating just thinking about it—may God grant that I never go through something like that again! It was all I could do to not fall dead to the ground.

I don't know who she is and why she did that. But I can tell you this: My grandchildren's father's aunt is one of those, you know, who uses those powers. My grandchildren's father is not a child of God, and my daughter has to face it. If the aunt knows it, why wouldn't he and all his relatives? They are from that area of Mexico where a lot of that evil goes on.

Did I go to a healer? Heavens, no! I don't want to get involved in that, the black magic—no! I just pray to God. The Almighty is the only One who will be able to put a stop to this. There is no other being who has the power to do it. No, no, none of that for me! God forbid! We are faithful people, believers and Christians. God forbid! Being spooked is pure horror!

I don't remember what happened after I was spooked. All I know is, I was taken to the hospital and was there for three weeks. I don't know what they thought, and I don't know what they did; I don't know what they were told, because I didn't even know who I was, I was that spooked. A tremendous, overwhelming fear that chilled my soul. I would say that my soul was hanging by a thread, almost leaving my body, you understand? It is a horrible, horrible sensation of fear, and panic, knowing someone truly evil wants to cause you harm and has spooked you.

The doctors think it is high blood pressure, but where does the high blood pressure come from, I'd like to know? I never had high blood pressure before, and I eat neither salt nor sugar, just as they instructed me. And sometimes when I lie in bed at dawn, the room starts to spin, and I can do nothing but cover my eyes and then look every few minutes to see if the room has stopped spinning. May God grant that you are never spooked. I don't wish it on anyone.

Stain

You can't imagine how it broke my heart to have my husband, whom I had always trusted, come home at midnight, supposedly from a friend's house, and say in an embarrassed voice that he was going to take a shower. I jumped up in a fury and grabbed onto him and demanded to know, why do you need to shower, for God's sake? What have you been doing? Show me, show me how you got so dirty, you filthy, disgusting pig!

He fought me off and yelled at me, told me I was crazy, but I kept him out of the shower by sheer brute force until I saw his underwear, and they were stained. You know what I mean—stained. And I started ripping at his hair and face and screaming at him, you this, you that, you filthy pig off the street! What do you think you are doing in this country? Have you fallen so low, away from your people? Is this who you are now? Is this who you have become?

Did you bring me here for this? Bring me here with our little baby so you could run around town like the—well, you don't want to know the word I called him—but, do you think I'm going to stay one more minute under your roof, you filthy, disgusting animal? He insisted he just had an accident and that it happens to men and I shouldn't make him embarrassed about it, like someone might pee their pants, and it happens to men, but people usually don't notice. But I had never heard of that before. I couldn't decide whether to believe him.

So I called the friend where he told me he had spent the evening, and the friend swore that my husband had been with him right up until he came home. He said they were just watching television and talking in a group of maybe seven guys. But then I talked to a sister-in-law who lives in that house, and she told me the guys had rented some of those pornographic movies. And they sat around in a group, the filthy pigs, and watched people having sex. People who are paid, who are not even real couples, just doing all kinds of sick things. I can't tell you how sick and sad it makes me. How can I let him touch me after that? It is nauseating.

And I know he was embarrassed, too, about the stain, about losing control and having the accident, and about watching those pornographic movies. You know how a man comes home, cheerful, and says, hey honey, I'm home; I brought this chicken; I brought this cheese for us to eat. This time, no, he came in with his head hanging in shame like a criminal and mumbled about wanting to take a shower. A shower at midnight! Does he really think I'm that naïve? He fought me off like a wild cat to try and hide the stain. But his face revealed his own guilt and shame, and I don't think he'll want to do it again. I don't think it was worth it for him.

Staying

The nicest thing for my wife is to know that I'm staying with her my whole life. Even now, when she has had the baby, and she is pretty helpless, she never has to worry about me leaving her. She knows I'll always be with her. We talked about this a lot before we got married. I'm staying for good. I will never, ever leave my family, no matter what.

We met here in the United States, and she didn't know my people and I didn't know hers, so she didn't know quite what to think of me. She was very adamant with me that she wanted a real marriage—both civil and religious ceremonies— and she wanted it to stick. I told her, guess what? I know how you feel, because my father left us, too, and I'm staying. I'll never leave.

Even before I met my wife, I had made the decision that kids need their fathers. They really need and want and love their fathers. And mostly, all they want is for him to keep staying around. For their fathers not to leave. So I promised myself, when I was still a child myself, that I would never leave my wife and children. And I won't. No matter what.

It is a good, solid feeling to know that only death will part us. She's not going to leave me just because I grow thin or lose my temper. I'm not going to leave her because she gets older and cranky. No. I'll stay and take care of her, always. She knows I will work two or even three jobs if I need to, to support my family. People leave each other for the dumbest reasons. What for? Then they just have to find someone else and get used to them. It's not going to be any easier, only harder with the new one. And the children suffer. I know I did.

My brother tried to say I'm planning too far ahead. How do I know I'm going to love her in ten or twenty years? But I do know it, because I know her. She can't change that much. Like me, I'm the same person I was the day I was born. A little bigger, of course. But the same person. So she will be the same person in fifty years as she is now, and that's the person I love. And I'm not going to change, either; I'll still be me.

My father, he tried to come back after two years. He begged and asked my mother to take him back. He said, the children need their father. Let me come back; I made a mistake. That was after two years of completely ignoring us, never visiting or even caring if we starved. But my mother said to him—and she said this in front of all us kids—What would I want with a man who leaves? And she found a man who stayed, later, and my father never got over it. Me, I won't have those problems, because I'm staying. She can't replace me if I don't leave, you see. And no one could take my place with this precious little one. She'll know what a real father is.

Stingy

I had a hard time living with my mother-in-law; she kept such a tight hold on the purse strings for the household. It wasn't like I was lazy, not at all. Believe me, I often worked side by side with my husband in the field. When I wasn't doing that, I was cooking the beans, milking the cow and goat, washing the clothes by hand, ironing clothes for the whole family, putting on the coffee, washing the dishes, making the fire, sweeping; whatever there was to do, I would do it. I did more work than a maid, but even a maid would get a small salary and clothing allowance and every other Sunday off. I got no time off, and no pay at all.

In the year I lived with her, she only bought me one dress. That was all the clothes I got for the year, and as to money, not a cent. I could eat what was served on my plate, but no more. I had no rights at all. I told my husband to ask his mother to give us some money. Let us go out and enjoy ourselves before the baby comes. What's the harm in spending a little to go dancing or visit friends? But he didn't dare ask his mother for money.

We never had any fun! My husband was very deferential to his parents and never really said a word about anything. Once we wanted to take a trip into town and he asked to use the truck, and his mother gave him such a tongue-lashing! What do you need to go to town for? You're not a bachelor anymore! You want to look for a woman?! Is that what you want? Well, too late; you have one right here and you brought her here, so you can stay here with her. If you wanted to run around, like I told your brothers, you should have remained a bachelor. That was her excuse, but it was all about the money. She was just so stingy!

And she wouldn't let me visit my parents or my people, either. She told me that she couldn't spare me; I had to work so they could make ends meet. Finally, after nearly a year of slaving away with no end in sight, growing skinnier day by day, I wrote to my brothers and asked them to take me away. They came and did, and they took me to the United States to work. I gave birth to my daughter here. You can't imagine how much I loved it! The luxury! Getting paid for my work, eating without asking permission! Having seconds and even thirds!

I didn't have to get up at dawn to stoke the fire or prepare breakfast for ten people. I slept in until my baby awoke. I worked eight hours a day, instead of sixteen or seventeen. And all my money, all my work, was for me and my little girl. I felt rich! Things were even easier when my husband gave in and joined me here. But now things are a little rough, because he wants us to go back to the farm, and I just can't face living with his stingy mother again.

Strain

I can tell the doctors how my daughter got her herniated umbilicus, if they want to know. We had a visitor who came over after work, and he works as a mechanic. I told him, go greet the baby. But he said, I can't, my hands are dirty. And he showed me his hands. Then he went to wash them. And I went in the kitchen to finish making dinner.

I didn't think anything more about it, and then we all ate dinner. I held my baby, and I saw she was straining. I just figured maybe she had a little newborn constipation. Sometimes that will happen—something the mother eats that doesn't agree with the baby. I saw her straining, and I gave her some chamomile tea to relieve her stomach.

The next day, I saw her umbilical cord, where it attaches to the stomach. And it was kind of red and not looking right. I kept checking it, and when I looked at it later, it looked like her belly button was pushing out, like the intestines underneath it were pushing through. It hadn't looked like that before, and that's when I called the doctor and made this appointment.

Now they are saying the baby may need surgery. It is hard for us to accept this. Because what we remembered later is this: Our visitor forgot to greet our baby. He went and washed his hands, and he scrubbed them clean. But then when he came out, my daughter was just sitting in her little infant seat in the living room, and he came right into the kitchen where all the good smells were coming from, and he helped me set the table, and then he was tired, and he sat down to eat. He didn't greet the baby at all. He is a good man; he loves babies, but he just forgot.

What we know is this: Babies need to be seen and recognized and acknowledged. And everyone who comes into a room where there is a baby, that person cannot ignore the baby. That person has to see the baby, touch the baby, look into the baby's eyes and recognize, acknowledge the baby. Then the baby can relax and feel normal. Then the baby doesn't have to strain.

If a baby is ignored, either on purpose or on accident, the baby will strain to be seen. If it is a boy, he can get herniated testicles. Sometimes, a testicle even gets sucked back in, and they call it a nondescended testicle. But it's from the strain. If it's a girl, she will strain and push to the point that her umbilicus will push out. If it is mild, she just gets a belly button that pokes out. If it is severe, like my baby, she gets a herniated umbilicus and needs surgery.

That is why it is very dangerous and bad to refuse to greet a baby, especially a newborn. They must be seen. They are not being selfish; it is something they really, really need. If you ignore them, they will have to strain to be seen, and it can be dangerous for them.

Stroke

They tell me I have aphasia. That means I cannot speak. I cannot make my tongue move around the words I want to say. They keep asking me, am I chewing gum? I'm not chewing gum. I can't stop chewing on my tongue. I chew circles on my tongue, trying to squeeze the words out of it, all the words I have stored since my stroke. But the words won't come out.

I know my son loves me. He isn't doing this to have me suffer. He is a young man, and he isn't ready to lose his mother. So now I will face this, on his signature. Wearing a diaper. A tunnel IV line into the neck. Amputation of my foot and part of my leg. The infection in the other foot; it will be next to go. Pain. Pain and ongoing dialysis until I finally die.

I am living in the nursing home now, when I am not in the hospital. They keep telling people, she has aphasia. You can talk to her, but she can't say anything back. She understands, but you can't understand her. Go ahead, talk to her. But people don't know how to talk to someone who can't say anything back. They don't want to look into my eyes. They worry, maybe, that I will ask something of them, ask something with my eyes that they won't understand, won't want to understand. So they say a few words, look away, and fall silent. The interpreter today, we had a long time together. She looked into my eyes. She explained things very carefully, like she couldn't tell how much I understood. Then she said this into my eyes: It must be hard for you, having all those words caught inside of you that you can't get out. I am sorry for your loss of speech. I wish I could help you, she said. I didn't say anything back. I moved my face, but nothing came out. My words are trapped deep inside.

Another nurse today, he held my hand and squeezed it, after they had tied me down for the procedure. One of the doctors got mad because I had broken the sterile field. I touched my face after they had washed me with the sterile soap, so they tied me down. They tied me down, and he washed me again, roughly. I didn't say anything, of course.

They had to put a tunnel IV line into my neck, so they can start my dialysis again and prepare me for the amputation. But they couldn't get the area numb. So I felt it when they were cutting and poking right near my heart. And I was tied down. And when I was chewing on my tongue, chewing it and wishing there was a way to squeeze the words out of it, the doctor saw me and got mad again and asked if I was chewing gum. I am not allowed to chew gum. But I wasn't, of course. I was chewing my tongue, over and over. I wish I could tell the doctors, tell my son, what I want. But I can't. So my son, and the doctors, will decide for me.

Taking Care

My husband has been taking care of me our whole marriage to avoid children. You know, withdrawing before—you know. But then we decided to have the baby, and after the baby came, the doctor told us we had to choose a real birth control method. Well, I wasn't willing to put something in my arm or inside my private parts and then end up having health problems. So I told the doctor, if I have to use another method, condoms would be the only thing I would use.

The doctor told me that condoms were a lot better than him taking care of me—you know, withdrawal. She talked about a single sperm swimming in and some other details. So I took home a brown paper bag of free condoms. I had them by the bed, and I told my husband, we are not allowed to have you take care of me anymore. We have to use condoms every time.

My husband was pretty hurt. He said it had worked fine for years, and why couldn't he just keep taking care of me like before? But I told him, look, the doctor says that I will get pregnant right away again if you keep taking care of me. She warned me it would be very bad for my health. So you can do what you want, use the condom or not, but you're not going to be touching me if you don't put it on, and that's final. And I stood my ground, like the doctor said.

He didn't like it, but he got used to it pretty well. I was the one who had the hardest time with it, since this creepy, plastic thing is going inside of me instead of just my husband. It doesn't feel the same. It's creepy, and it doesn't slip around. So I finally decided, I can't stand it anymore, but we're not allowed to use our method, so I'll just give up and get the Depo-Provera shot and hope I don't get sick from it. I mean, it's not like you can take it out again; it's a shot.

That's when I came to the clinic and got the pregnancy test and it was positive. And I told the doctor, my husband is really mad at me and says it's all my fault we got pregnant, since I insisted on using condoms instead of letting him take care of me. And the doctor just laughed and said the only way you can get pregnant on condoms is if you don't use them right. And she told me the same story about how one single sperm can swim up and all those details. And she asked my husband, were you putting the condom on before everything started and not taking it off until everything ended?

Well, we weren't, but he always put it on before the last moment, and I don't really understand how we could get pregnant doing that when he took care of me for four years, and nothing ever happened. Maybe you just get more fertile after you have a baby. Anyway, now we have another nine months to decide on another method of birth control, besides condoms.

Taxi

Since I had the Cesarean and the baby is still in the hospital, they told me my medical insurance included a taxi to visit my baby and bring in my breast milk. I only need a taxi on days when my husband works. When he is home, he drives me to the hospital and stays most of the day, too. But I had so many problems with the taxi lady, I have been taking the bus, and I think that's why I got that infection in the surgery scar, from carrying the cooler with the breast milk and standing for a long time where I have to transfer buses. The bus ride is rough on me.

I called the number you gave me for the taxi, and they put me on the phone with the Spanish-speaking lady. I told her I wanted a taxi from Monday to Thursday, and she started laughing at me, like she was making fun of me, and said, who is going to feed your baby on weekends? I told her, my husband takes me in on weekends. And she asked, well, why can't your husband take you in on weekdays, too? And I told her, because he has to work on the other days.

So then she asked me, why doesn't he take you before work and pick you up after work? And I told her, he works two jobs and I have to take the kids to school, and that's why I can't come in at five in the morning when he goes to work, and then she asked me, well, who feeds your baby at night? So I told her I use a breast pump and bring the milk to the hospital in a cooler like the nurses told me I could, because my baby is so sick and tiny, she can only have a few drops of milk at a time. She can't even have a whole ounce at a time yet.

Anyway, she just kept asking me questions and more questions, and then she said she couldn't send me a taxi for 9:30 a.m. after I got my children to school because I had to accept the taxi whenever they had time to send one, since I didn't have a real appointment. I was so surprised, I didn't know what to say, so then she asked me, well, do you want a taxi or not; you'd better just make up your mind, and I said, well, with the way things are, I guess I don't want a taxi, because I can't leave my kindergartener at home alone and just leave when the taxi comes; I have to get him to school first. Then she acted like I had wasted her time, and she hung up.

Then the hospital social worker told me that the taxi lady had no right to ask me anything except where I was going and when I needed to go and my address, but all the rest of it was none of her business. I didn't know; I thought she was like a doctor or nurse and could just ask me anything she wanted. The social worker told me to call her back and tell her I want a taxi, but I just can't make myself do it. Could you or someone else call her for me? I mean, it's nice to know what my rights are and everything, but I just can't. I can't face talking to her again.

Thin

I'm embarrassed to tell the doctor this, but I can tell you. I don't have enough to eat. I think that might be why my baby wants to come out early. It's not that I'm ungrateful for the help; I really am. That's why I don't want to complain. But my husband couldn't find a job for a long time, and so the WIC checks were really all we had for food. And you know, we have the two kids besides this unexpected one, and they need the food more than we grown-ups do.

Here's what we've been doing. My husband has been working a few shifts at Burger King. They let him eat there, but they don't let him bring home food. So when he works, he eats as much as he can hold. Then he doesn't eat anything at home at all. He saves up his hunger until he works again. He says it doesn't bother him to wait a long time to eat, since he's a man.

Through WIC, I get a certain amount of cheese, milk, cereal, and peanut butter; they call it Women, Infants, and Children. It's like the extra food that the other people don't want or something, like if they have too many cows? But they don't want to kill the leftover cows, so they milk them and give the milk to poor people's children. Something like that, anyway, is what the WIC lady told me. Same thing with the cheese. I don't know if they have extra peanuts, too, or if they just want new people in the country to get used to peanut butter, since we don't eat it at home. At least I've never seen it before.

Okay. So I get the cheese, milk, cereal, and peanut butter. But it seems like they are thinking, hey, here's a little snack for you. Add this to your diet, like a vitamin pill. But guess what? My husband's whole paycheck goes to the rent and only some of the utilities. We are behind on the electricity or another bill every month. Then when they say they will shut it off, we pay that one and can't pay the other ones. We can't buy much food at all.

So the WIC food, I have to make it last. And this is how I am doing it. I am making a nice, big bowl of hot cereal, and I eat it in the middle of the day when I'm already very hungry. Then I pour a glass of milk, and I drink that in the evening when I'm very hungry. Then all the rest of the cereal, milk, cheese, and peanut butter, we buy crackers to eat with them and we let the kids share all of that. When my husband gets a better job or a second job, then we can start having regular meals again.

So if you can find a nice way to tell the doctor, maybe she can just feed me the hospital dinner and send me home, and I will quit contracting. I'm a little embarrassed to tell her myself. I don't want her scolding me. And tell her I promise to try to eat more just as soon as I can.

Thirteen

I was thirteen when I got married. No, it wasn't in Mexico. People would think that, but it was in southern California. I was just a girl, really, but I was old enough that my parents let me go to a dance under the supervision of my big sister. I was so excited! I got all dressed up in the nicest dress I had, the one I wore on Sundays, and my sister put my hair up, and I even wore makeup and perfume. I was nervous with joy.

Well, the dance was filled with a lot of young men, needless to say; there are many more young men than girls who come here to work. I danced and danced and danced. Then a grown man, he asked us if he could accompany us home. He was someone we had seen at our house visiting my auntie, so we said yes. Then we stopped by his apartment on the way home.

I probably shouldn't have done this, but he offered me my first taste of beer. I drank two of them, and then he sat by me on the couch. My sister was hinting to me that we had to leave, but I was so happy. He was treating me like a real grown-up, like I heard older ladies talking about. He put his arm around me and kept telling me how beautiful I am, and how much he liked me, and he tickled me and he—well, I guess he might have fondled me just a little bit.

He left us a ways from our door, and when we got in, my father was waiting for us in a fury. He demanded to know everything. My big sister tried to say nothing, but he beat it out of her, then he beat it out of me, anyway. Then he took his rifle and visited that man, and then he came home. I was never so scared in my life as I was when my dad told me that I was going to marry that man as soon as they could get the license arranged!

I told my mom once we were alone, please, Mami, nothing bad happened. You can check me, check me like they do the bad girls, take me to the doctor, it would be worth it to prove it to you; I am still whole. But she said it was too late. She just shook her head sadly at me and told me I was getting married. There was nothing she could do. The deal was made.

Well, I never saw that man until a week later when they took me to the courthouse in the same Sunday dress. I just stood there crying as they made me sign the license and they witnessed it. My parents wrote that I was sixteen. The judge probably just never saw someone cry so much, but they say a lot of brides cry for joy, and so how could the judge know I didn't want this? I couldn't speak enough English to tell the judge, and my dad was right there anyway. After that, I had three children and lived with my husband until he left me. It wasn't easy to live with a man who married you under a death threat, but that's all over now, thank God.

Threat

I'm a soccer coach. And there's always going to be someone who says I'm too passionate, too intense, too demanding. Because when the kids don't work hard, I get pissed off. I want them to want to win more than I want them to win. And I want to win a lot. These aren't little kids anymore. These are young people now. And they need to decide what they want, and they need to work for it. They have to work for it. And I'm going to make them work for it.

If they don't work for it, I'm going to squeeze them off the team. Not to punish them or hurt their feelings, but for the good of the team. I call it shaking the tree. I shake the tree, shake them up, to see who falls off. Who is holding tight to the goals and aspirations of the team as a whole? Those ones, they won't let go. They won't fall off. The ones with the weakest grip, either poor skills or moral weakness, they let go; they fall off.

This one weaker player, his dad is a cop, you know. So he has this certain don't-fuck-with-me-I-have-a-gun attitude. But I'm Salvadoran. That's the last thing in the world that is going to intimidate me. You have a gun? So what? You know how many times I've had a gun held to my head without showing any fear? No, you don't, because you're a dumb-fuck cop from the U.S., and you don't even know where my country is; you don't know shit. So that's my internal dialogue with the cop, the conversation in my head. You see?

So when he found out I was looking to replace his son, and he started threatening me, it meant nothing to me. It meant less than nothing. And he wasn't joking. He made direct, physical threats, but I didn't care. He warned that I would face pain and embarrassment if I didn't quit coaching. He threatened to physically remove me at the next game! But he didn't get it. To say that, to say that to a Salvadoran, you might as well just tell him to do the opposite.

All I could do was laugh and shake my head at his ignorance. He really has no idea who I am or where I am from, or even his own history. He thinks I'm some wimpy little scared white guy who's going to tremble in my boots and give up the whole team just because he scares me, that I am not going to do what is right for the team just because he's a cop and he has a gun.

I am Salvadoran. That's what he doesn't get. I'm Salvadoran, and you could have ten cops and torture me and pistol-whip me and interrogate me and torture me some more, and you could never, ever, ever make me do what I don't think is right. We don't cave in. Fuck everybody, no offense intended, but Salvadorans don't cave in for anyone anywhere, ever. And no dumb-fuck white cop from some backward town in the U.S. is going break me. Ever.

Toe

I am a grown man, even if I am a young guy, and it must seem like I'm being a baby to cry about this, but we Mexicans like to be buried whole and complete. You know, the Second Coming and all that? Well, we really believe it, and we want to die with all our parts. That way, when I do come back to face the Final Judgment, I won't be limping or incomplete.

You probably think it's silly, but it's just this big taboo for us to have missing parts, even if it is just my big toe. I think it will be harder for me to, you know, marry and everything. I mean, there's nothing pretty about a guy with one arm; he might be a great guy, but he doesn't seem whole. He's missing something, and he couldn't protect a woman the same as a two-armed man. You might feel sorry for a one-armed man, but you wouldn't want to marry him.

I just moved to the U.S. to help my mom; she has been struggling to support us kids and I wanted to help her out. I just got here and I heard about the Millionaire's Club, and they have this work program. It's easy. You just go stand outside the club as early as you can, and you look like you're ready to work. Then people drive by, and they say, like, eight, and you know they mean eight dollars an hour. Then they say, like, all day, and you know they will have you work the whole day, which is good.

So this guy who owns a big warehouse, he picked me up for three days in a row to carry boxes around and load trucks and stuff. The first two days, they had a guy supervising who was Mexican, and I could understand him fine, of course. But today, they had an Asian guy giving orders, and he was new, too, and he was trying to speak English, and I was trying to understand his English, and it wasn't working.

He started lifting the platform we were standing on to load a truck, and it started to rise up into the air to the level of the truck bed, except my tennis shoe was caught in the crack by the toe, and my toe was caught and getting ripped off my foot. No one could really understand right away, so my toe was mostly ripped off when they finally shut off the machine.

Sorry to be such a baby. It's momentary weakness. I understand this doctor; they could sew it back on, but since it's smashed up and pulled off, it could get gangrene or something, and I could lose a bigger chunk of foot, or even the leg. So I'll try to be brave about it. I want to get back to work as soon as possible. I just hope I don't walk with a limp, because then it will be hard to get work. And hard to get married, someday. You use your big toe to walk, you know.

I know it probably seems like a toe is a small thing, but it is my big toe, and I'll miss it.

Tooth

My husband is hard to understand; he is just learning to talk again since his brain damage, but yes, you did understand him. He got the brain damage from his molar. Yes, that's right. He got a cavity, you see, and we couldn't afford to get it filled right away, since it is expensive. We were getting onto a program called Medicaid where they help you with doctor and dentist bills, but then we found out it was only for children. So they told us to sign up for something called Basic Health, but then there was a long wait list and when my husband got to the top of the wait list and got the coupon, we found out that Basic Health does not pay anything for dentists.

By then, many months had gone by, and the tooth was really hurting him. We got money together from friends and family; it is hard because we are all migrant workers and we don't have a steady income and sometimes we don't have any income at all, but we always have to pay our bills, or we can lose things like our place to live or our electricity. And then the dentist said my husband needed something called a root canal and a crown, and those two things together were going to cost more than two thousand dollars! We offered to pay a hundred a month for two years, or just pay to pull the tooth, but the dentist said he didn't like to pull teeth, and he couldn't afford to take payments and he was sorry, but we should try to find a clinic.

We called all around, but there are so many people in need, and mostly they are just interested in helping children now. I think they are tired of helping grown-ups, or maybe there are just too many of us. So no one could help my husband, and his whole jaw swelled up, and we didn't want to go to the emergency room because they get mad about people coming in and they would have told us to go to a dentist, but no dentist would take payments that we could find, so my husband just tried to handle the pain and we put clove oil on the tooth, but then he collapsed in the field one day.

The doctor here explained that his infected tooth infected the jaw. That was why his cheek and neck swelled up. Then the infection got into the throat and down into the lungs, and his lungs collapsed, and that was when he fell from the ladder. And people tried to help him, but he didn't have enough oxygen until he got to the hospital, so he got brain damage. So they flew him to Seattle, and now he has been in the hospital for three months.

The strangest thing is, our Basic Health insurance will pay for his brain damage, his hospital stay, all his therapy and care, but they wouldn't pay for the tooth. Isn't that the strangest thing? And now that he can't work, he can get Medicare, they tell us, the good kind of coupon.

Trade

Since I can remember, probably since I was a kid, I used to sit around in Cuba and think about living in the United States. I used to sit and think I would trade it all for money, you know what I mean? Trade everything I had. We never had enough. We always had to be so careful. We never ate in a restaurant. We never had new clothes. We never had a car. We didn't even always have a fridge that worked, and we never had a washer of our own.

I heard about a lot of people who left, people we knew, and they would travel back to visit us, through Mexico, and I would see what they had. New clothes, all brand new. New everything; even their suitcases were new. Pictures of their places in the States, their cars, their everything nice. And I put myself in that picture. My own little North American Dream.

So I moved here. I traded everything, so to speak, and moved to Seattle. And I worked two jobs, working my ass off, but loving it. I wasn't raised to be afraid of hard work; I was raised to work! So everybody loved me at both my jobs, and I made a lot of money. And for the first time in my life, I had money. I had more money than I had ever thought I would. I had extra money, money I didn't need for anything. And I had credit, and credit cards.

I sent my mother all the money she asked for, whatever she needed. I bought myself a car, a brand-new one, no money down and just make payments. I started going out to eat, buying nice clothes. I got myself a really nice apartment and bought nice furniture, and then guess what?

I finally had everything I always thought I wanted, and I found out it isn't that great. My apartment, my new car, my clothes, my everything I bought. It just wasn't worth it. I finally realized I had traded everything, traded every single thing in my life, for money.

My mother, my sisters and brothers, my neighbors, my childhood friends, my house, my yard, my town, my food, my plants and flowers, my ocean, my weather, my education, my language. My culture. My island. My life. I had traded it all, every single bit of it, for money. And with all that money, I couldn't buy back a single thing of all the things I had traded away. Things of value have no price, as I found out. But it was too late, and now I can't go back.

That's when I got depressed and lost one of my jobs and got behind on the rent and built up that credit-card debt and defaulted on the car loan. I'm still driving the car; they can't repossess it because they can't find me, since I lost my apartment. Isn't that ironic? I traded everything for money, and now I don't have any money. Welcome to the North American Dream. And everyone here thinks things are bad in Cuba. They just don't know. I didn't.

Transportation

Can you help us get permission to transport our twins to California for burial? See, we don't have the money to fly them, like the rule says. But the social worker yesterday said you can get a special permit from someone to take a body in your own car across state lines.

It's not that we don't like it here in Washington. Not at all. It's just that we're new here, and we don't have any people. The closest people we have are in California, and we have some of our dead buried there. We thought the babies might be less lonely among our own people. They wouldn't have anyone here. No one to visit their little graves.

We would stay here, to be with them, but we don't have that option. Since we work the fields, we have to move around. We have to follow the crops. But my people in California, they're always around. So the twins won't be all alone all the time; they could have visitors.

If we can get work, we can settle there, too, and if God grants us—well, I don't want to talk about it in front of the twins. They are the only children we're thinking about right now. So if we can settle there, stay with family and find work, we can stay with the babies.

Tell the lady who decides, we will do whatever she says. Like the ice, or the special boxes, or what have you. And we will just drive straight through, only stopping for gas, if there is a time limit on how long you can take to drive there. We don't know what all the rules are. We never had dead babies before. This is all new to us.

I asked the doctor, but he said to ask the undertaker. About the one twin's head. It's kind of crushed in, like it caved in? I wonder if his face could be made to look more even and round for the funeral. The doctor said to ask the undertaker, since he will prepare the bodies for transportation. It's just that my people will only see these babies once, at the funeral, and we want them to look their best. We want people to love them. They'll only meet this once.

We have nice outfits for them to wear that are really cute. Someone gave them to us at our baby shower. They are complete with little socks and booties and hats and everything. They are a little big, since the babies are so premature, but they're very beautiful outfits. I think they told us the babies could wear whatever we wanted for the funeral. That's nice, so they get a chance to wear their best clothes. So people can see them in their best light.

I guess we just feel like if we can get the twins transported back to our people, they won't be as far away from us as they are right now. It will make them seem closer to all of us. So I hope they will let us drive them there in our car. Can you please find out for us?

Undissipated Rage

You want me to explain what the interpreter wrote down on the form, under cause of death for my father? Yes, that's what I told her to write. It says Undissipated Rage, right? Isn't that a cause of death in the United States? You want to change it to heart attack? But undissipated rage is a different thing.

My father, may he rest in peace, was a good man. Like any normal human being, he would get mad sometimes, but he wouldn't yell or raise a hand to anybody. He would just get mad inside and hold it in. That's not good for your health. That can hurt you.

My sister, she was going out with this boy my father really liked, from our neighborhood. We all figured they would probably get married eventually. But that summer, a guy we didn't know, who had lived in the United States, came to visit our village with our cousin, because they had been fishing together in Alaska.

Because of our cousin, the guy started spending a lot of time in our house. He talked a lot about how much money he made, how he loved living in the United States, and how everything was better there. He talked about how he liked coming to his home country, but only to visit, and how he liked to travel around, instead of always just visiting his family.

My father didn't like him. He didn't like his ways. But my sister, she started to like him a lot. She was impressed with him and his independent talk. So after a while, she told her boyfriend to quit coming over; she started being busy when he wanted to do things with her. And she started spending more time with the guy who lived in the United States. But my father, he never said anything about it. He just held it in.

After the guy left, we were all kind of relieved, but then my sister told my father that they were engaged, with no respect shown. My father didn't say much about it, but we know him, and we could tell how furious he was about it. That night, we all heard him pacing and sitting up in the rocker, and in the morning, he was dead in his rocker. But the doctor said he didn't have a heart attack or a stroke; he said it was undissipated rage.

I can't believe you don't know about undissipated rage in the United States. It seems like people hold in their feelings so much here, it would be a real common disease. I guess you call it all heart attack, that must be why it's the leading cause of death in this country—they said on television. Somebody should look into that. Anyway, the nurse can write whatever she wants on the form, but that's what he died from. Undissipated rage.

Unforgiven

My daughter is alone in Mexico now, and she is suffering. I might feel sorry for her, but I have hardened my heart. The family says she cries a lot and is very repentant, but of course that is how she is feeling now when she has to support herself and face the consequences of her actions. Now she has a child of her own, and that ended her childhood. I warned her. It's a shame, but I don't forgive her, and I won't forgive her. I don't forgive either one of them. God is punishing them both, praise Him in His wisdom. Me, my conscience is clear.

My daughter, she lived with me, and we were all peaceful and loving until I let this man move in. Who would have known that one lone man could cause such suffering? Now I know what you're thinking. You're thinking, he must have molested my girl, abused her, but it wasn't like that. She fought me for him. She fought me for him like a woman.

He lived with me for a year and then took all his belongings and said he was moving out, and I should ask my daughter why. I did ask her, and she was defiant and rebellious as she told me she was going with him, that he loved her best, that she was pregnant and they were going to get married and form a family and have nothing to do with me. She told me I was just an old woman and he never loved me and he only wanted her all along.

I gave her a chance, in spite of my grief. I told her, you are just a child; you don't know what you're doing. He took advantage of you. Let's stay together. I will forgive you and still mother you, and we will care for the child together; but she said no. He didn't take advantage; he just loves me better, and I hate you for ever having been with him, old woman. That's what she said to me. Well, we'll see who's an old woman now. She'll look my age soon enough.

She left with him in spite of my pleas. He never did marry her, of course. I offered her one last chance to come home and be a child, but she just laughed at me. She made fun of me. Everyone was talking about it, and how taken in I had been. I had done everything a mother can do, and she only despised me for it, so I closed the door on her forever.

He left her, of course, as I knew he would. Him? He got another young girl pregnant, from another family, this time a fourteen-year-old, and he's in jail for it. My daughter, she got deported to Mexico and has to work all day long to support her baby. A teenager with a baby is no one there. There's no pride in it, only humiliation. The family says she cries herself to sleep at night and berates herself for not staying with me. Now she is all alone, and for the first time in years, in her proud heart, she cries out for her Mami. But she is unforgiven. Let her suffer.

Virgin

I was in a very bad marriage. He seemed nice enough, but after we were married, he became terribly jealous and controlling, and he began to beat me. So when I left him and found this younger man, this nice man, I was so happy! I didn't think it through, and I agreed to have a baby with him out of wedlock. So I have my two kids from my marriage, and now this baby.

My boyfriend's father, he says he accepts the baby as his grandson, especially since it is the only grandson so far. He says this baby will always be his first grandson. But he says he will never accept me as a daughter-in-law—even if we marry— because I was a used woman. I was not whole, he says, because I was not a virgin. So he is very opposed to his son marrying me or even spending much time with me. He has to visit me on the sly. And now things are worse.

My boyfriend's mother is very ill, or maybe she isn't. I don't know. But my boyfriend was sent back to Mexico, since he is the oldest son, to take care of his mother. Or maybe not, since I can't be sure she is truly ill. They say it's her heart. And now I am hearing through friends that he is looking for a fifteen- to sixteen-year-old virgin to marry from his village. And I don't know if that's just talk from his father to scare me or make me jealous, or if it is true.

My boyfriend calls me from Mexico every few weeks. He's been gone four months now. But when I've tried to get a clear answer from him, he just laughs at me on the phone and says, you're not going to get all jealous on me now, are you? But he neither confirms nor denies the rumors I have heard through our friends. Then he said he will talk to me when he gets back, and I said, about what? What do you have to tell me that you can't tell me on the phone?

So I ended up telling him, look, you do what you need to do. The last thing I want is to force you to marry me and then get the crap beat out of me again for years. There's no point to it. I won't force you into anything. I won't make you mad, and I won't obligate you to anything. I won't slit my wrists, and I won't blow my brains out. But I think that since I provided you with a son, the least you can do is to tell me straight out: Are you looking to marry someone else? Are you leaving me? Or are you planning to come back to me? But he still wouldn't say.

Then I told him, your father thinks you shouldn't marry me because I was married before and have children by another man. But what makes you think some pretty young virgin, fresh from the nuns, is going to want you when you already have a child? You're not that young yourself. And you have a family already, just like I did when you met me. So you're not such a great catch. Me, I'm only with you because I love you so much. But I won't force you to stay.

154

Warm

I surely do love having a Latin husband. I know some of my friends from work, they married white men to get papers, or maybe because they just wanted something different, or maybe they just loved them, I don't know. But I know this: None of their husbands have nearly the warmth and affectionate nature that my husband does. I'm so glad I married him!

Take our childbirth, for example. Did those other husbands bring their wife flowers? Sure, a few chrysanthemums without a real card. Did they stay there during childbirth? Well, yes, sitting in the corner watching television. Did they get their mother to come live with them a month or two after the birth? Of course not; their mothers are all busy working. Now take my husband. He's from Guatemala. And he's so affectionate, I almost can't stand it!

My husband didn't just bring me a couple dried-up flowers when I gave birth. No, it was a dozen red roses. Do you know how much a dozen red roses cost? It's a lot. But he didn't care. He thought I deserved them. And he wrote a card. And the card said how much he treasures me. How beautiful I am to him. How much his heart beats only for me, and I am his heart and his soul and his life's companion, and how much he welcomes our baby.

What did my husband do during the birth? He sat in the bed with me. He rubbed my back. He brought a wet washcloth to my forehead. He pinched my ears and stroked my eyebrows. He got tears in his eyes when the pain was bad, and he hugged me and held me and let me bite his shoulder whenever I wanted to. Not every man in the world is going to allow that.

Did he bring his mother to help us? Yes, he did. And she cooked and cleaned, and all I had to do was be pretty and take care of the baby, that's what he told me my job was. For forty days! Of course, I helped my mother-in-law, but think of all that comfort and help!

My husband holds me in his arms every single night. He can't get enough of me. He sniffs me and rubs his face against me, and he breathes me in and licks my neck. He simply adores me. He is so affectionate, and he talks all the time about how much he appreciates and loves and adores me. Sometimes, he'll get home from work and he'll fall on his knees in front of me, and then he'll grab me around the waist and he'll hold onto me tight and bury his head in my bosom and just tell me over and over, he loves me, he loves me, he loves me.

And he means it, because he shows it to me every day. That's why I feel so lucky. I know that every culture has loving men in it, but there's some special kind of an open-heart thing that comes from the way we mother our boys that is above and beyond. Our boys adore women.

Water

My water broke at six months of pregnancy; that's how he got this way. I used to cry about it so much, my sisters all scolded me. All a mother wants, if you get right down to it, is to protect her young, that's all. And when you can't do that, it's hard to feel grateful. It's hard to feel okay. So I cried about it a lot. I know it's wrong, but I couldn't help myself.

When my water broke, I spent a few weeks in the hospital with them pumping liquids in, and me pouring them back out, and then finally the doctors said you just have to deliver; there's nothing we can do. That's why he can't walk or talk, and he has the eye problem. And asthma. And his legs go all crooked even with the braces on his feet.

We waited a long time, maybe a year, before he could get in and see the experts. Now they have done eye surgery, and both his eyes look in the same direction. Now that he's a patient here, I can bring him here for emergencies, like when he has bad asthma attacks.

It was in the emergency room here that I first learned to feel grateful. After all, my baby has all his parts; he isn't missing anything. He can usually breathe pretty well, except when he gets his asthma attacks. But he doesn't need a tube to breathe, and nobody has to suction him, since he can swallow. And he can eat anything he wants; he is a good eater.

I've seen kids who can't do anything, really, kids who will die or who will live, but in a lot worse shape than mine. You know—you've seen them, too. They're all over the hospital. And they all have mothers, too, every single one of them. Crooked, twisted kids with missing parts. Kids who couldn't look you in the eye, even after an eye surgery like my boy's. My boy can look me in the eye. He has all his parts. He is whole. And I know he loves me.

With so many kids worse off than mine, I see how truly lucky I am. I see all the bald babies who aren't going to make it. They suffer so much, the poor little ones. Mine doesn't seem to have much pain. He plays so nicely with his big brother. So I thank God and I am grateful that my boy doesn't have even more wrong with him, like some of the other kids I see here. I thank God that he doesn't have a fatal disease like leukemia. I thank God he isn't blind like they said he might be. I thank God that he doesn't have worse breathing problems. And that he is whole and complete with no missing pieces. And capable of giving and receiving love.

But God forgive me, when we're not at the hospital, when we're home alone, I still sometimes wish my water hadn't broken when I was six months pregnant. And I feel guilty that I can't be more grateful. And I pray for resignation.

Weapon

I had a small shop in my home in El Salvador. Pretty much every block had a little neighborhood store, run out of someone's yard or front room. Neighbors could buy some basic items, like milk, cheese, ice cream, soda, eggs, and bread. And we were the ones in our neighborhood that had that kind of a store, so people thought we had money, and probably guns. A lot of stores had guns for their protection, but we don't believe in that, so we didn't.

When the guerrillas first started to be active in the city, at the beginning of the civil war, it was pretty scary. They were just boys, really, schoolboys, and they were as scared as we were. They didn't know what they were doing, and I know they felt bad about what they were doing—robbing and stealing in the name of the poor. Then one evening, they came into our home.

I should say our yard, because you know, that neighborhood, we all had ten-foot walls around the houses and the yard was like an inner courtyard. The guerrillas came in through the store and came into the yard. And we were home alone, me and the children, since my husband was traveling. I can't tell you how afraid I was. My older children were in the house, and only the little one was keeping me company at the store.

We were just closing up the store when they let themselves in. They burst in with submachine guns that were bigger than they were—just teenage boys with scarves over their mouths and soft, beardless cheeks, who tried to sound tough when they insisted, give us your arms! In the name of the poor! Make it quick! Give us all your arms from the whole house now, or we'll kill the both of you! Their voices were trembling with fear.

I looked them over and saw they were just boys who went to school with my children. And as scared as I was, I forced myself to figure out who was their leader. And I looked right at him and looked him in the eye with my daughter behind me, and I said, in the strongest voice I could muster, we are decent Christian folk. Our only weapon, our only defense, the only arms we have for our protection is the Bible, and the Holy God who wrote it. And I pulled the Bible off the counter of my store and I started to hold it up to them, and they stepped back.

Then I started to sing a Christian song, and my daughter joined in with her trembling voice, and soon we sounded stronger, and I saw one of the boys wipe away a tear and one of them told the leader, who was standing there, come on, let's go; they don't have anything. And they went back out; they didn't even ask us for our money. When my husband got back, that's when we decided to leave the country. All these years later, I still pray for those boys every day.

Wheelchair

We were going to move to California, because there is no work in Washington for farmworkers now. But my husband said no. Our son has spina bifida—where your spine doesn't close right—and for a while he could use a walker, but now we have to carry him everywhere. It took us many months before he could get to a doctor, so my husband said we can't move to California, for our son's sake. You see, we are on a wait list here for a used wheelchair and if we move, we have to start all over again.

I told the public school, I am unemployed now. I can come to school with my six-year-old and carry him around. They said no, you can't enroll him if he doesn't have a wheelchair. We are not set up to help someone like your son, they told us. So he hasn't been able to go to school yet. We have been here for two years now, but it took a long time to get in to a doctor.

He was getting physical therapy in Mexico, but then we lost our jobs and they wouldn't take payments, so they cut us off. That's when he lost his ability to walk, when he wasn't getting the exercises and medicines. At home, we tried to copy the therapy we saw them do at the clinic, but we don't know as much as the therapists, and it didn't work. We talked it over as a family and decided it would be best to come to the United States and work to get more money.

That's how we got here, and the first thing we did is try to find out how we can get any medical insurance, but I guess with what they call temporary work, there is no medical insurance they'll let you buy in Washington state, so we asked for what you call Medicaid, but now they say President Bush doesn't like immigrants because of the building in New York and the airplanes, so he is taking Medicaid away from all the little children who were not born in the United States; even very sick children are being cut off from help, and that includes our son.

See this letter? The neurodevelopmental doctor here wrote to the farmworkers' clinic. He says, "I complimented the mother for obviously being so vigilant in her son's care." That's nice, but I would like to get a wheelchair for my son so he doesn't have to stay home another year. We can make payments; we don't mind working hard—we're used to that—but it seems nobody trusts us to let us have one that way. I am his mother and I carry him everywhere, but he is six years old and growing fast. I can't carry him forever. That saying in the Bible—he ain't heavy, he's my brother? I believe in the Bible, of course, but that boy must not have been paralyzed from the waist down, because a paralyzed child is really, really heavy.

White Girl

I am sure he fired me because he saw me kiss that white girl. See, my boss, he had made a comment at work, like to each his own, I'm not racist, but stick to your own kind. I told him, man, you don't get it. Mexicans are not one kind; we have Spaniards, who brought Portuguese and Blacks and Arabs and Jews, and Indians from five hundred tribes, and Europeans, and even some Chinese and Japanese who also settled there, and this century, the Nazis and the gringos. We have very beautiful people. Mixing the races, it makes for beauty.

He didn't like it, but he didn't say anything more about it. I thought he had dropped it. I don't know, maybe he liked this girl himself, but if so, he should have told me instead of talking about it like she's a German Shepherd and I'm a Mexican Chihuahua, and he's the dog breeder.

So we were in this bar, before Christmas, and it was like our company party, and we were drinking. We played pool and listened to music and drank a lot of beer and ate some good food. Some of the white guys who work there, they don't like us all that much, since we work so hard and they want to earn a lot, but not work hard, and then they get told, like, look at Juan, Mike; why don't you do it like him? So there's some resentment there. I'm not saying everyone is like that; some of the people, they're like me. They get along with everyone and just do a good job and make friends easily. I'm not saying all white people are lazy. Some are hardworking.

My boss, he isn't so friendly. I myself thought that he shouldn't have come to the party, or at least he shouldn't have stayed. Because this white girl, she kept kind of following me around, you know? And he kept following us around, like, trying to talk to her. So then I would move away, and she would follow me, and he would follow us. So, like, he went in the bathroom and when he came out, we had sat at two bar stools, and she was telling me how beautiful and thick my hair is, and she says, you look like you could use a haircut, and I say, I don't have time, and she says, what are you so busy doing, something like this? And she grabs my hair in both hands and pulls me to her, and she kisses me by taking my bottom lip in her mouth.

And why lie? I liked it—I liked it a lot—and I kissed her back. I never met a woman who would dare to just grab you by the hair and have her way with you. I felt like I died and went to heaven. I didn't even see my boss come out of the bathroom. I forgot his very existence. But the next day, the boss called me and said I didn't get along well with the others, and he fired me. The funny thing is, this girl, this white girl? She said I could stay with her while I look for a job, and I doubt that's what the boss wanted to have happen. But you know what? We're not dogs.

Widow

My daughter doesn't understand. She wants to support me by coming to all my doctor's appointments, but she is impatient and she interrupts me and she contradicts what I am trying to tell the doctor. If I try and tell him how my vision is poorer, she will say it seems like I walk around the house just fine. If I tell him I've been in more pain, she will interrupt and say I haven't been complaining of it at home, and she thinks we should just keep going with the radiation and not give me any days off. Only I know what I feel, and what I suffer in silence.

You're young. Your husband is still with you. You can't imagine what it is to walk through this world alone, no one to hear your cries at night, no one to comfort you. I hold so much in. I hardly ever tell my daughter how bad I feel. Why should I? If I ever do, she scolds me and tells me I'm being negative, that I'm always complaining and should just buck up and keep a positive attitude. She doesn't know half the pain, no, not a tenth of what I suffer.

It is human nature to complain. You won't find a psychiatrist in the world who will tell you that it is bad to complain. Not one who would advise against getting things off your chest. But we can't all afford doctors. Most of us just talk to our life companions, our husbands. And then men have to go and die earlier than women, and where does that leave us? A decade, maybe longer, with no one to share our burdens. I've been a widow nearly a decade already, and these have truly been the hardest years of my life. I have cried my eyes out.

My husband was a brilliant man, may he rest in peace. What an intellectual! He would have laughed at this cancer with me. He would have listened to my complaints and tried to alleviate my suffering, instead of belittling it. He would have found all the right books to read aloud to me at night. Now that my eyesight is growing dim, I can't even enjoy reading, which was my chief pleasure. My daughter tells me to just watch television. Television! Good God.

My daughter married wrong and got divorced. I think that's why she never really understood what it meant to me to lose her father. She was always so independent and never really bonded with her husband, and then they separated. She doesn't know. She doesn't understand that I don't need her to push me into further treatment or contradict me at the doctor's, or scold me to shut up and try harder. What a woman at my time of life needs is a strong arm to lean on, and that is the one thing I am lacking since I buried my beloved husband.

I am eternally bereft, and I know she loves me in her own way, but she really doesn't know the first thing about what I am going through. Really. Not the first thing.

Work

In California, I worked sewing uniforms. It was in a big factory, and we had to sew very, very quickly. They didn't pay much, and your pay depended on how fast you could go. The fabric was newly cut and as I ran the pieces through the sewing machine, the fabric dust would fly up into my face. They didn't have very good ventilation, and the dust was everywhere. It was horrible. I put up with it for years because I was just so glad to have work.

Then I started to get nosebleeds. I would wake up in the night with blood on my face. If I sneezed or coughed hard or rubbed my nose, blood would just start pouring out. I went to the doctor, and they sent me to an expert. He put this long, long thing up into my nostril; it seemed like it was going up into my brain. And he took something out, or he burned something, and then he told me, you have to change your work. The more dust you inhale, the worse your symptoms will be, and it will never get better if you don't change your work.

That's when I moved to Seattle and found this job. I looked all over California and couldn't find anything. The economy was already slow. But up here, it was still good when I came three years ago, and I was able to find a job processing fish in a plant. I feel lucky to have a job now, when so many people are looking. Even people who speak English are having a hard time now, from what I've heard. I don't think that happens very often. It must be scary for white people to look for work over and over, like immigrants do, and not find anything.

I'm glad for the work, but my hands ache all the time. It hurts your bones to have your hands freezing cold all day. We can't warm up, because then the fish would spoil. We have to be cold, and stand all day, and use our hands. I rub my hands a lot to try and get the blood back into them. I feel like I'm getting arthritis in the joints of my hands from all the work. But I have to work. And without English, I don't have many options. Thank God I have my health.

I never think about not working; it's not an option, because I support my elderly mother and my young daughter back home. I send them money every month, because almost everyone there is unemployed. A young girl and an old lady can't find any work. Everybody needs money. I'm just grateful to live somewhere where a fifty-two-year-old woman can still get work. There aren't many places like that in the world. That's what I tell myself when my legs get tired from standing or my hands start to ache. It could be worse. I know it could, because I have lived through worse things. Sorry to cry; I'm not crying for myself, but for my mother and my daughter. It's so hard on them when they can't find work. Thank God I can still work.

WorkFirst

I have worked by my husband side by side in the fields during all of our twenty-five-year marriage, right up until two years ago, when I noticed the changes. I had more and more trouble feeling my hands and being able to shut them. My fingertips starting turning purple in the cold, and my skin grew thick. I got spots on my chest and neck. I started to hurt a lot.

My husband, he got me to a doctor, and they said I have an autoimmune disease. They say it's a disease where your skin and connective tissues inside your body—like the outside layer of your heart, lungs, intestines, stomach—they start to get hard and turn into a stiff, thick, scar tissue. I was able to slow the disease down with shots and pills, until the lady at Social Services cut off my medical benefits and I had to quit going to the doctor for a year. Then things got bad.

She said there was a new program called WorkFirst, and I had to take classes to become a secretary, or she would cut off my benefits. I tried to go, but I can't close my hand or hold a pencil because of my disease, and I can't sit for very long with the pain. Also, I never had the chance to go to school, either, so I can't read or write. I would love to learn a trade, or be able to do a job, but I don't think my body will let me anymore. I told her this, but she didn't believe it. She said I couldn't get any help unless I tried harder. She cut off my medical care.

A nurse where we live, she found out the caseworker had cut off my benefits. She fought for us and we went through the appeal, and a year later, I got my medical care back. But since I went a year without the steroids and other medicines, my skin has grown a lot thicker. It's hard to open my mouth, and swallowing is also painful now. Also, breathing is harder, and the doctors say my lungs have now gotten scarred. I know that lady didn't mean any harm—she was just doing her job—but I wish she could have known me a little better. Maybe she could have taken the time to listen to me, or talk to my doctor. He knew my condition.

If she had known me, she would know what a hard worker I am. She would know that I am used to working in the fields from dawn to dusk and still coming home to cook for seven people and then do laundry half the night if need be. Our house was also as clean as I could make it, and we had nice meals and good, decent children who went to school and never got in trouble. Now I am stuck home alone all day, wandering around the house like a lost soul, unable even to sweep with my broken hands, and every time I try to cook or do dishes, I cut or burn myself. I wish God had opened her eyes. Then maybe I would still be able to take care of my family. Instead, pain greets me every morning and waits for me at night, and I am helpless.

Young

Well, you're not the first one to ask. But if you think I look young for my age, you should see my bride. We've been married for 52 years, but you'd sure never know it by looking at her. She's such a young, pretty little thing. Sure, I'll tell you how we did it. I don't guarantee that it would work for anyone else, but I can tell you how we did things.

I think the secret to staying young is to stay calm. Don't let yourself get ruffled. Don't let yourself worry about the morrow, like they say in the Bible. Were there times when we had things to worry about, like weather or farming troubles? Sure, there were. But instead of worrying too much, we just left all that in the hands of God, and counted our blessings.

It takes us a long time to count all our blessings, so that stops us from having too much time to worry. For example, at our time of life, what do we have? We have a wonderful farm that our youngest son runs. We have two children living in the United States who send us some extra money to help us out. They also fly us here to visit them every other year. We have two other living children with very nice jobs. They are all married. They all get along. They are all healthy. We have grandchildren and even great-grandchildren living right on the farm, so we never lack for company.

I think that's about it. We never had too much, but we never had too little. And living on a farm—even a small one—there's just something about looking around and seeing land, seeing land that is under your care. It's a good, solid feeling. You see things die back, and you see them come again in the spring. Same thing with the animals. You have the slaughter, but there are always animals left to carry on, and it just carries on into the future, with no end in sight.

I think that people who only think about their own lives, who see themselves as separate, are the ones who grow old quickly. You see them here, those ones. Worried, wrinkled old ladies, even though they can't be that old, hurrying their children into car seats to rush them to day care. Balding and scared-looking old men, maybe only twenty-five years old, running to cross the streets downtown at noontime. Hurrying along, all alone in the world, old before their time.

See, people here don't stay close to their families. They get divorced, and they don't even spend time with their own parents. How can you stay young when you're so alone, so hurried? When you're not a part of the whole thing, the great union of things that carries on into the future?

So if you really want my advice, you'd better take care you don't get caught up in it, madame. You look pretty young now, but that could change anytime. Look around you.